Don't Tell Me
It's Impossible
Until After
I've Already
Done It

Don't Tell Me It's Impossible Until After I've Already Done It

PAM LONTOS

WILLIAM MORROW AND COMPANY, INC.

NEW YORK

Library of Congress Cataloging-in-Publication Data

Lontos, Pam.
   Don't tell me it's impossible until after I've already done it.

   1. Success.   2. Lontos, Pam.   I. Title.
BJ1611.2.L66   1986   158′.1   86-5185
ISBN 0-688-04893-5

Printed in the United States of America

First Edition

1 2 3 4 5 6 7 8 9 10

BOOK DESIGN BY PATRICE FODERO

*To Zig and Jean Ziglar, who had faith in me
and led me to have total faith in God—
the Highest Power, who watches over us
and is always there to make all our dreams
come true when we open our hearts*

*To Anna-Marie and Ryan, who bring
happiness into my life*

Grateful acknowledgment is made
to Carlton Stowers and Betsy Cenedella,
who contributed so much to the
final shaping of this book.

Introduction

It was one of those pitch-black nights that the man who worked security at the railroad yard had come to hate. The dark brought uncertainty, a sense of not knowing what waited ahead, and he disliked it passionately—almost as much as he disliked the responsibility of entering the refrigerated railcars used to transport perishable goods. There, the cold turned the dreaded darkness into something almost tangible. Though he admitted it to no one, the cold and darkness terrified him for reasons he could not explain.

He was nearing the welcome end of his rounds and had put off going into the refrigerator car until the last minute. The silent dread weighed on him more heavily than usual as he wearily climbed inside to make sure all was in order.

Then, just seconds before he had completed his duties and would be ready to return to the warmth of his well-lit office, he heard a sound that struck in him a numbing note of terror.

He was aware of what had happened even before shining his flashlight in the direction of the heavily insulated car door. The door had slammed shut, locking him in, alone. He knew the door could not be opened from the inside. And there was no one on the outside to call to for help. He was trapped. Doomed.

He would die there, he knew, either from the cold or from lack of air. It was the thought of freezing to death that concerned him most. He screamed until his lungs burned and banged on the door until his hands were swollen and bruised. In time, however, the panic subsided and a resolution unlike any he'd ever felt set in. His situation was hopeless, his fate written.

He decided his last act would be to record his agonizing death for whoever might eventually find him. Taking a pencil from his jacket pocket, he wrote on the car wall: "It is so cold in here I can hardly stand it. . . ."

After a while he struggled from the corner where he had huddled and wrote a second line: "It's colder still . . . my fingers are getting numb."

Then, later: "I'm slowly freezing to death. . . ."

And ultimately: "These are probably my last words. . . ." By the time he had scribbled his final sentence, the writing was almost illegible, the hand of a dying man.

It was the following morning when his body was found, slumped in one corner of the refrigerator car.

The coronor had great difficulty determining the cause of death. There had, he determined, been sufficient ventilation inside the car to allow a man to survive for days. And, since the refrigeration apparatus of the car had been out of order, there was no way the man could have frozen to death.

In fact, the temperature inside the car when it was finally opened was fifty-six degrees.

* * *

The moral of the story is clear. The security man, burdened by fears and self-doubts, had become the victim of the awesome power of his subconscious. He expected the worst and, unfortunately, saw those expectations realized. Rather than making a positive and optimistic assessment of his situation and seeking some way to get through the nightmare, he gave up. He surrendered to a reality that existed only in his mind.

The price he paid, obviously, was the highest that humankind has to gamble. But his dilemma—his insecurity, his inability to sweep aside his feeling of hopelessness—is not that different from problems that millions of us deal with day in and day out.

I know. I've been there. Figuratively speaking, I've feared the same dark and I've felt the cold when it wasn't really there. I spent a lot of years looking at life from a dangerously negative vantage point.

But that was another time. I've also been fortunate enough to see it from the other side—and learned how much the human spirit can accomplish with nothing more than a simple belief in self.

Which is what this book is all about. It is not a book of magic. There are no shortcuts to instant happiness and success. I'll even go so far as to admit that reading this book won't guarantee an immediate change in your life. That's up to you.

What I have attempted to provide is a working outline, a guide to steer you in the right direction, to point the way toward a fuller, more rewarding and productive way of living. I call it the Formula of Success.

I developed it myself, living it day by day, moving, slowly at first, then by leaps and bounds, from one extreme to the other. And as I look back, tracing the progress I've managed, the recurring thought that comes to mind is that it's really not that difficult. Particularly after you've taken the first few hard steps to get the momentum—and motivation—headed in the right direction.

The limitations we place on ourselves are only in our minds. It is the negative thoughts—which may be entirely untrue—that keep us from achieving what we want, whether our goal is a happy marriage or the million-dollar round table.

For years I lived with those limitations, allowing them to stop me before I even dared start. I was too quick to believe what others were telling me.

Until one day I adopted a new attitude, a new philosophy. I came up with an answer that I felt perfectly fit my new approach to life:

I told them: "Don't tell me it's impossible until after I've already done it."

And if you truly believe it and put it into action, it will work for you!

PART ONE

1

There was a time, not that long ago, when the idea of speaking my mind, even at a small gathering, was the most frightening prospect I could imagine. In the first place, I was dead certain I had nothing of worth to contribute, either to a serious discussion or to light, chatty conversation; in the second place, I would have stumbled all over my tongue even if I had found the courage to speak out.

I'm the person who, as a child, was a constant embarrassment to a mother justifiably concerned by my shyness. I'm the person who froze with stage fright during my brief career as a high school teacher, and flatly refused to stand before a group of seven fellow teachers, simply to ask for volunteers to handle refreshments for an upcoming school function. In all honesty, I would have given up my job first. I'm the person who went to absurdly elaborate ends to avoid placing myself in any kind of social situation.

It was more comfortable to stay at home, safely isolated from the challenges and confrontations the real world offered. At home the demands were simpler, and I could handle them. Or so I thought. What it boiled down to was that I was hiding from the world behind a wall of self-doubt, rock-bottom self-image, and fear of failure. And to complicate my situation, I didn't even recognize the fix I was in.

I wasn't living; I was surviving. I wasn't really contributing, just tagging along from day to day.

It was a way of life in which I had formed the habit of existing to my negative thought patterns, long before reaching adulthood.

My purpose here is not to force upon you the life story of Pam Lontos. If, in fact, you are curious enough to be reading this book, I have to assume that the person you're most interested in is you. Certainly I hope that's true. Mind you, I'm not endorsing a "Me Generation" philosophy. However, you must be confident and love yourself before you can be of help to others. Deal with your own insecurities and recognizing your hidden potential are the first steps toward attaining the goals that I sincerely hope this book will help you to reach. Each one of you is unique and what you want out of life is different—to be a better parent, mate, employee or boss. Perhaps some of you desire more recognition, success, love. But whatever your desire is, the end result should be happiness for you and those around you.

To make my point, however, I feel it important that you know something about me and how I have become the person I am: not perfect by any means, not even the ultimate example. But believe me when I tell you I'm far happier with myself than I was just a few short years ago. And things are still getting better—which is the part I like best. The negatives are now gone from my life, stored away in a past that was, to put it mildly, a struggle. Today, one of the things that excites me most is the prospect of tomorrow.

Such hasn't always been the case.

My father was in Europe, fighting in World War II, when I was born. I was almost a year old before he first saw me. And when he did, I think it's safe to say my presence wasn't greeted as that magic blessing the romantic fiction writers would have us believe.

He had returned home with the dream of becoming an internationally famous artist, a man who would have to serve no other. A fierce artistic independence burned in him.

But as soon as he settled into civilian life, with a family he had not had before entering the service, he was greeted by the two-dollar woes of day-to-day living. There were bills to pay, mouths to feed, obligations to be met on the first and fifteenth of every month. Though his desire to be a famous artist never died, he was forced to view the world more realistically. A paycheck was needed, and thus he put aside his dream and worked at doing murals on restaurant walls and helping with the interior designs for a variety of buildings in Dallas.

The kind of personal satisfaction he so deeply craved was seldom realized and he did little to hide his disappointment. There would be lengthy stretches, in fact, when he would simply stay at home, waiting for work to come to him. If it did, fine. If not, that seemed okay too.

One of the first things I remember his telling me was that had it not been for me, he would have achieved his ambition to become a famous artist. Though too young to understand all the adult trials and tribulations involved in being a breadwinner, I did manage to come to one quick realization: My presence had more or less ruined my father's life. It caused me great difficulty, because I loved him dearly. And, in his own way, he loved me. In fact, I considered him my closest and dearest friend until the day he died. Still, the underlying feeling of guilt—that I had robbed him of his dream—always weighed on me.

Born in Greece, he was a man who held firmly to the Old World traditions. Even as I grew to school age he seldom allowed me to attend parties or spend much time with other kids. While my contemporaries were dating and talking on the phone for hours, I was rarely allowed to go out with a boy, unless he was a member of the church—and then only to select church functions. Even then, any boy who wanted to take me out had first to meet my father and gain his approval. I had a strict five-minute limit on telephone calls, incoming or outgoing. There was little, if any, flexibility in my father's rules. And there were, it seemed, a lot of rules.

Forced to spend most of my time at home, I became a firsthand witness to the seemingly endless mood changes that characterized the relationship between my parents. Constantly aware that one of those dinner-table verbal sparrings could break out at the slightest provocation, and last at times until the wee hours of the morning, I was always on guard. The ability to interpret their moods, to foresee the emotional explosions before they actually occurred, provided me with knowledge of how I should act around my parents. My chief guard against involvement was to retreat to my room, there to read or listen to the radio.

I made those retreats often, and became something of an expert at invisibility.

On the other hand, there would be times when my father, having wearied of fighting and seen my mother to bed, would call me out for long talks and games of Scrabble. Those, frankly, were the best of times. He never talked to me as to a child, but rather shared his thoughts as though I were his equal.

By the time I was twelve years old I had come to at least one fairly adult realization about my father: I was afraid of him, of his moods, which ranged from depression to giddy delight, from anger to near serenity. I was afraid of him almost as much as I loved him.

I feared him; I loved him. And I wanted his approval more than anything in the world.

Though not yet even a teenager, I looked much older and decided to try to use that fact to my advantage. It was less than four months after my twelfth birthday that I applied for a Christmas-season job in a Dallas dime store and was hired. The job was beneficial in many ways, not the least of which was that the $1.25-an-hour I was earning enabled us to purchase Christmas gifts we would not otherwise have had. Equally important to me was that my father, who did not hand out approval without proper justification, exhibited such a positive reaction when I turned most of my paycheck over to him that I was encouraged to continue with the job after school hours once the holiday season was ended.

I had worked hard all my life—in the most literal sense—for his approval and had finally found a way to get it.

By the time I was fourteen I was selling shoes at a neighborhood discount store, working on a commission basis. I worked weekends and on Thursday nights, selling $12 shoes for 10 percent commission. There were days when I sold as much as $300 to $500 worth of shoes.

The more I earned, the more dependent the family became on my financial support. That my father worked only sporadically, content to use my income for whatever immediate household needs arose, really didn't bother me. Why should it? That he was praising me for my efforts, showing me more and more attention, was reward beyond my wildest dreams.

With the feeling of accomplishment and the praise, however, came a new form of stress, one I had no way of anticipating.

When a call would come, threatening to turn off the water if the long-overdue bill was not paid immediately, it fell to me to plead our case. Same with the irate calls from an impatient landlord. Neither my father nor my mother would deal with the problems, simply turning them over to me. They assumed, I suppose, that if I was old enough to be a wage earner, I was old enough to attend to the other financial problems of the household.

How I hated it. Still shy and withdrawn, confident only in my ability to sell shoes and make reasonably good grades, I dreaded the stress that accompanied my attempts to persuade that person on the phone not to throw us out of our house, or threats of a march on our home by collection agency officials.

With the benefit of adult retrospect, I realize now there were legitimate reasons why I should have felt at least some degree of self-confidence as a young girl. After all, I had managed to get a job and to help with the family income at an age when most aren't even thinking of such things. There were pluses to be recorded in my ledger, but I just didn't recognize them.

Criticisms—the minuses—pointed out to me regularly at home, at school, and within my limited social circle, so overwhelmed the positives that they were never real to me.

My mother, a perfectionist, pointed out my flaws in a sincere attempt to help me develop into the kind of young lady she felt I should be. When I returned from grade school with a report card filled with C's and D's she scolded me. Her disappointment was evident. It was obvious to me that I simply wasn't growing up to be the kind of person she so desperately wanted me to be. Instead of being brilliant and witty, the kind of daughter every mother wants, I was a poor student and shy to a degree that perplexed her.

The impression I was making away from home wasn't much better. Teachers, I was certain, had decided I was a slow learner. And because of the limits my father placed on my social activities, I had no real friends and was viewed by my classmates as the ultimate wallflower. I was the last picked for teams on the playground and therefore quickly lost interest in group activities.

I was getting nowhere in a roaring hurry and had not the slightest idea how to resolve the problem. In fact, I didn't even recognize that there was a problem. Which is to say, I wasn't seeing things too clearly. Again, I'm speaking both literally and figuratively.

I was in the fifth grade before it was determined that I needed glasses; that maybe, just maybe, some of the academic problems I'd long struggled with were not the result of nonfunctioning gray matter but of terrible eyesight.

For years I had gone to movies thinking that the screen was filled with little more than fast-moving psychedelic colors. The voices were clear; so was the music. But the faces were always a blur. And since I had seen things that way from the day I first opened my eyes, I had no frame of reference to indicate that it should be any other way.

At a young age each of us creates our own universe, and everything therein evolves from our inner selves. You'll pardon my play on words, but we blindly perceive the world in our own fashion and simply assume that others share the same view. It just never occurred to me that others might see things more clearly.

It seemed natural to me that all trees, when in bloom, looked like big green lollipops. I had no idea the leaves had definition and depth and so many different color tones. I experienced no frustration at being unable immediately to distinguish one face from another when visitors entered our living room. Everyone, I assumed, had difficulty telling a dog from a cat.

Even now I can vividly recall the day it was first discovered that I needed glasses. A large eye chart was placed at one end of the classroom and all the students were told to line up near the blackboard at the opposite end of the room. When it came my turn to read the chart I wasn't able to get so much as the first letter. There were a few snickers from my classmates and some bewildered looks from the teacher and nurses giving the test. Not only was I unable to read the largest letter at the very top of the chart, but one of the teachers had to show me where the chart itself was located.

When I was later taken to an eye doctor, it was determined that I had 20/400 vision. Legally, I was blind.

Up to that time, I don't think any of my teachers suspected that eye problems might have something to do with my poor grades. Since I was well-behaved and created no problems, they must have assumed I was a sweet little girl who was, unfortunately, just plain stupid.

Then there was that agonizing period between the discovery of my sight problems and my getting glasses which caused me additional problems. My teachers, in an attempt to help, removed me from the rest of the class, placing my desk near the blackboard. It was as if I had been exiled, singled out, and it embarrassed me greatly. I felt as if I was on exhibit, and wished desperately to be able to disappear back into the group.

When I finally put my glasses on for the first time, it was as if I were visiting some marvelous new planet. Suddenly I was seeing things I'd never even imagined before. I was stunned by the clarity of things. As my mother drove me home, I remember how surprised she was that I repeatedly commented on all the billboards along the way. She couldn't understand it. I was carrying on like a person who had never seen them before—and she knew we had traveled that route hundreds of times. The fact of the matter was, though, I was seeing them for the first time.

In only six weeks my grades improved to straight A's.

This is the point in the story where everything is supposed to turn out happily ever after, right? The shy little girl who has been a loner and a poor student suddenly becomes the most popular, the highest achiever in the class, right? Unfortunately, it just doesn't work that way if you're a person who has developed an uncanny knack for taking two steps backward immediately after taking one step forward.

Though my glasses afforded me first-time looks at a number of fascinating things, they also forced me into a world I was neither prepared for nor interested in joining. The fact is, I became more self-conscious than ever.

Vanity played its role. I had never considered myself pretty and now my self-esteem was further lowered by my being forced to wear glasses. Suddenly I was able to see clearly into the faces of those I judged to be beautiful and those who no doubt recognized that I wasn't. But I soon found a way to hide. By taking my glasses off, I could retreat into my more comfortable blurred world.

I was like the baby who covers his eyes, certain that no one can see him.

2

The foundation upon which one's success is built is formed from a mixture of several ingredients. A positive self-image is, of course, essential. So, too, is a reasonably wise range of experience. I can't think of a single person who has attained any measurable degree of success in business or day-to-day living who hasn't formed a courageous belief in himself or herself and been willing to take those chances that broaden horizons and expand awareness of one's own capabilities.

I'm reminded of a man who, for several years, was considered one of the best young editors in New York publishing circles. Carefully he would smooth away the rough edges of the prose written by some of the world's finest authors. The publishing house where he worked considered him one of its most promising employees and rewarded him with high praise and a good salary. But there came a time when working on other people's books no longer provided the personal satisfaction for which he longed. He wished to be a writer himself, to see his own name on book jackets in the windows of New York's leading bookstores. He had, in fact, begun work on a novel while in the service and had completed it during his spare time. When the company he worked for agreed to publish it, a giant step was taken toward the new career he so eagerly aspired to.

By the time the book was in the marketplace he was already at work on another and approached his boss with the admission that he wanted to spend a greater amount of his time as a writer. He proposed an arrangement whereby he would work as an editor half of each day, then be allowed to devote the remainder of the day to his own writing.

The executive frowned, concerned that one of his editors might be working only part time. "You're a good editor," he said, "with a promising future in this business. Why would you want to throw that all away to try and be a writer? I read your book. Frankly, it's not really that good."

The aspiring young author, stunned by this criticism of his firstborn, asked, "Why would you even publish the book if you didn't think it was any good?"

"Because you work for us and we felt by publishing the book we could keep you happy, that's all. Nothing more, nothing less. Your future is as an editor, not a writer, believe me."

Angered, the aspiring author admitted that he had a second book nearing completion and would offer it to some other publisher just as soon as it was finished. That exchange, which took place on a Monday, brought to an end the working relationship between the promising editor and the New York publishing house.

Two days later *The New York Times* reported that the newly unemployed editor had been selected as winner of the Pulitzer Prize for his first novel, *Tales of the South Pacific.*

* * *

That's how James Michener, one of the most successful, most gifted, and most highly respected authors in modern literary history, began his career. Turning his back on the negative thoughts of others, he held to his strong belief in himself. That solid self-image gave him the courage to broaden his creative canvas and step beyond the security of a job that failed to offer him the challenge he needed.

We are all a bit richer for his willingness to take that chance. And, while not all of us are candidates for literary fame and fortune, we can certainly learn from the dedicated approach of the James Micheners of the world.

It is the rare individual who is able to venture alone into those uncharted areas where experience is to be gained. For most of us, the decision to risk failure for the possibility of success takes a little shove, a little encouragement now and then. Otherwise, we go along our safe accustomed pathways, never taking the turning that might lead to realization of some hidden potential, some talent or gift that hasn't been given a chance.

I was in junior high when a school party was planned at the lake. The entire class was scheduled to go for an enjoyable day of picnics, games, and swimming to celebrate the end of our eighth-grade school year.

My mother would not allow me to go; at best, I was a poor swimmer. Even though I promised not to go into the water, she flatly refused. I might drown, she said. So, while the rest of the class went off to the lake I sat alone in a study hall all day. Risk taking, I was taught, was foolish.

To this day I can't swim very well. But one of my new goals is to learn.

When I was a youngster, though, such an ambition would have been judged foolhardy by my parents. The slightest venture toward something new and different was looked on with disfavor. When other teenagers would leave the neighborhood for a Saturday shopping trip, they were criticized by my parents. Never mind that they were only going a few short blocks away. It was foolish, dangerous. And, though I wished desperately to join them, I could only assume that my parents knew best what I should and shouldn't do.

Virtually any kind of social involvement, I came to believe, was a risk not to be taken. If it did not revolve around the activities of the Greek Orthodox Church and those who attended, I did not take part. As a result, my feeling of isolation, my sense that I was different from most of my peers, became even stronger. There was something wrong with me, I knew, but I wasn't sure what—except that I was dead certain I was one of the world's original ugly ducklings, unpopular, not at all pretty, and scared to death of trying to match wits with anyone my own age.

Recently, for reasons best described as nostalgic, I pulled out a scrapbook of photos of me as a youngster and came to a long-overdue realization. I'm not going to say I was the Brooke Shields of the sixties, but I wasn't nearly as homely as I had thought for all those years. The truth of the matter, actually, was that I wasn't at all ugly.

Then I looked at photographs of those girls I had thought to be so beautiful and the boys I knew to be far too handsome ever to give me a second look. Sure, they were nice-looking, smiling beneath their flattop haircuts, but it wasn't their features that struck me as I looked back into the past. On each face was a look of confidence. I saw a lot of warm, friendly faces, not a gallery of potential high-fashion models and Robert Redford threats.

I was thirty years old when I came to that realization.

Why hadn't I been able to understand that I could have fit into the crowd from which I felt so isolated? Why hadn't I realized that I, too, had the potential for popularity and enjoyable, fulfilling relationships? Why hadn't I been able to look into the mirror and see that I was not the unattractive person I thought myself to be?

Again much of the blame has to be placed on the workings of the subconscious mind. Whatever the subconscious holds is, whether you realize it or not, your dominant thought. It feeds on itself and if that thought is negative and you refuse to break away from it, things have but one direction to go: from bad to worse.

If James Michener had felt about his first book as did his boss-publisher, he would never have completed it, much less seen it win the Pulitzer Prize.

As those around me began dating, I felt even further removed from the social mainstream. Because of my shyness, I had never spent much time around boys my age. As a result, there were precious few calls at the Congas house from anyone who might have wanted me to see a movie or go out for a hamburger with him.

Those who did call were quickly dissuaded from making it a habit, since my father had a standing, unbendable rule that anyone who wished to take me out had to meet him first and gain his approval.

More than once I can remember boys' gathering the nerve to come by for a meeting with my father, only to be told that he did not wish them to call again. He would give no reason, simply stating that he would not allow me to go out with them. Period.

As you can imagine, word of such rejection spread quickly. Even those who might have wanted to ask me for a date weren't about to subject themselves to the cross-examination they knew they would have to undergo. Even though I really wasn't ugly, I wasn't worth all that. It was far less trouble to ask some other girl who had a less demanding father and who could at least talk on the phone for more than five minutes.

To rebel against such restrictions never entered my mind. It would have gained me nothing but the same flat *no* many of my friends had heard. So I dutifully accepted my role as an outsider and did the best I could to hide the hurt and anger I felt.

It seemed that every aspect of my life compounded the lack of self-worth I was dealing with.

While, as I've mentioned, we were light-years removed from wealth, the geographic location of our home was such that I had to attend a high school whose enrollment consisted mostly of youngsters from affluent families. Many of the students drove their own cars and wore clothes far nicer than mine. In my mind, every school day was a fashion show and I had absolutely no business stepping onto the runway. No matter how carefully I prepared my wardrobe, I knew I wasn't going to look as fashionable as the other girls. It was a battle lost before I ever went to my closet. In fact, if my fondest wish had been granted, I would have been invisible.

Which is to say my high school days weren't the happy, carefree times they were supposed to be. In truth, I was miserable most of the time.

It was, I suppose, nothing more than curiosity that drew me to the twentieth reunion of my graduating class a few years ago. Like most, I wanted to see if the beautiful girls had become beautiful women, if the sons of rich fathers had become richer in their adult lives. And I was curious to see how I was remembered.

What I found was that I was hardly remembered at all. One man, whom I recalled as one of the most popular boys in our class, came up to me at the reception and introduced himself. We talked for several minutes; then he said, "Boy, I wish we'd had somebody like you in our class." It was, no doubt, part of a well-rehearsed line, but it was flattering nonetheless.

I smiled and said, "I was in your class."

He looked at me with a surprised expression on his face. "Really?"

There I was, the same person in the company of the same people I had known twenty years earlier, but few recognized me. It wasn't that I had grown into some gorgeous woman who stopped conversation simply by walking into a room. The difference was that I had developed an openness, a smile, and a friendly air that invited others into my world. The shy, fearful Pam Congas was gone, replaced by a woman of confidence, a person eager to make new friends and join the conversation.

Those few who did remember me were just as stunned as those who could have sworn they had never seen me before. There were a couple of men who had very flattering things to say. "You know," one told me, "I always wanted to ask you out, but I was afraid to because you never would even speak to me." And there were those who admitted that fear of my father had kept them away.

What I now realize is that a lot of my problems were self-inflicted. Because I was shy and avoided others, they were hesitant to approach me. They didn't recognize the poor self-image, the doubts and the shyness. Instead, they saw a young girl who appeared cold and not interested in being a part of their group.

Add to that the parental restrictions of my youth and you can see why the gulf between my peers and me seemed to grow wider with each passing year. And as that gulf widened, the image I had of myself continued to deteriorate. Pessimism bound me, holding me back from virtually everything I wanted to do. I saw others driving their own cars when I didn't even know how to drive; wearing fine clothes when I could not afford the price of a new skirt; being far more independent than I was, and able to carry on conversations I would not have dared enter into. They were all the things I wanted to be but hadn't the slightest idea how to become.

I was so filled with negative thoughts that I placed binding restrictions on myself. I had not yet reached the realization that one's personal limitations are mainly the product of one's own mind. I had not recognized the simple fact that I had as much potential, as much right to be accepted as anyone else; that I could not only cope with life but find it enjoyable.

I lacked the courage to venture past imagined boundaries on my own. And my parents, not understanding my desire to be a part of the world I watched from a distance, refused, for whatever reason, to provide the necessary push that might have started me in the direction of my dreams. Rather, they held too tightly, too protectively.

It began to occur to me that the only way I would ever break free of those bonds was to leave home and attempt to start a life of my own. As I grew older I thought of it often, always imagining the wonders that would ensue, once I was free to make my own decisions and chart my own course.

As I would find out, freedom is a difficult thing to acquire.

3

The summer following my senior year in high school, I was leaving church one evening when a man approached whom I had first met when I was ten years old. He smiled and asked if I had graduated from high school. It was a question he had asked me in passing on several previous occasions but I thought nothing about it. He was, I assumed, simply being cordial to a young girl who seemed to have little to say to others at gatherings.

More than a little proud of the fact, I told him that I had finally received my diploma, and then began outlining my plans to enroll at Southern Methodist University the following fall.

For the first time in my life I was feeling twinges of independence, and the anticipation was exciting. Since I would be paying my own way to college, funding my education with money I was earning selling shoes, there was little argument my parents could justifiably advance. My mother, to be sure, had made it clear she felt I was making a mistake by investing all I earned in tuition and fees, but I was determined to go to college. I saw it not only as a way to improve myself but as at least the first step in an escape from the day-to-day drudgery of my life. My entire world had revolved around home, church, and work. I was certain that on a college campus, there awaited some great new adventure: a new start. And I looked forward to it, counting the summer days until time to enroll.

The man to whom I was confiding my educational plans was already well on his way toward his own career goal: He was studying to become an orthodontist. He was twenty-eight, pleasant, and handsome. And, for reasons I didn't completely understand, he seemed interested in me.

Several days later he stopped by the store while I was working and asked if I was planning to attend the party scheduled at the church that evening. He offered to give me a ride. Flattered, I told him that my parents were taking me. I didn't want to explain to a twenty-eight-old adult that my father had an unbending rule about prior approval of anyone I went out with—even for nothing more than a ride to and from the local Greek Orthodox Church.

I was stunned when he returned just minutes later to tell me he had called my father and had been told it would be fine if I went with him to the party.

I called home to verify the news and was surprised to hear my father enthusiastically telling me to go—and to have a good time.

Thus began my relationship with Ernest, a man ten years my senior, a man who would eventually become my husband.

The truth of the matter is, my father knew I would marry Ernest long before I did. In time I found out that he had told several of his friends that "my daughter will marry the person I choose for her."

Obviously, he had chosen Ernest.

The Greek tradition of women marrying older men was something my father believed in strongly. That Ernest was Greek and working toward a successful career made him ideal. Add the fact that his personality was a perfect complement to my father's, and he had all the requirements for a son-in-law.

Ernest was quiet and reserved, offering no social competition to my father's outgoing dominance of a conversation. Anyone who emerged as a rival to my father's living-room storytelling was immediately dismissed as brash and far too overbearing.

Because of the comfortable relationship Ernest enjoyed with my parents, the summer following my senior year was one of the pleasantest I had ever experienced. Whenever he called to ask me to a movie or a concert or a party, my parents quickly urged me to go. If a party lasted past midnight, I would routinely call home and be immediately told not to worry about it; to stay and enjoy myself.

At the time, I was too naïve to recognize the reason for my parents' new attitude. All I understood was that Ernest, because of the favor he had found with my father, provided me a freedom I'd never dreamed possible. It was a wonderful feeling.

Ernest brought a new harmony to my life. To be able to leave the house without a litany of do's and don'ts was nice. And I was as impressed as my parents were by Ernest's quiet seriousness, by his never raising his voice, by his saving and working toward the future. I felt good with him, away from the countless demands and loud arguments of home.

Ernest became my escape that summer. I so enjoyed being with him that it never occurred to me that our personalities were poles apart, that we were about as incompatible a couple as one could imagine. That just didn't seem important, weighed against the delight of being allowed to go out freely for the first time in my life.

*   *   *

My enrollment at Southern Methodist University the following fall opened wide the door to a new world. Though
the campus was just a few short miles from home, it offered a life-style and attitude and atmosphere remarkably
different from anything to which I had ever been exposed.
Like all college environments, it was something of a melt-
ing pot of society: a collection of students from varied
backgrounds, different geographic areas, new and exciting ideas. I wanted to take it all in at once, breathe in the
exciting, refreshing atmosphere in one hungry gulp.

Throughout my academic life I had associated with the
same group of people, through grade school, junior high,
and high school. During that time there had been no last-
ing friendships, little participation in school activities, and
very few dates. I didn't even have a date to the Senior Prom.

But on that very first day on a college campus an attrac-
tive young man, also an incoming freshman, approached
me, introduced himself, and asked if I was interested in
going to a fraternity party with him that evening. He was
a member of the freshman football team. And though I
turned down his invitation with some now-forgotten ex-
cuse I suddenly felt like Cinderella.

I'm not suggesting that I took the SMU campus by storm,
stealing hearts right and left, but it was immediately obvious to me that some of the boys were attracted to me
and interested in getting to know me. I was mystified by
it all but at the same time, warmed. What, I wondered,
had suddenly made me different? Why had the people I
had gone to high school with never shown the slightest
interest, when all of a sudden my fellow college students
found me appealing?

Again, I was struggling with a self-image problem.
Throughout my junior high and high school years I had
been bashful and had backed away from the crowd because of the negative feelings I had about myself. Estab-

lishing myself as judge and jury of my own self-worth, I had determined that I was an outsider. And those who had grown up with me, from grade school on, had accepted my evaluation as theirs. These new people, however, didn't know me, hadn't been exposed to my shyness and standoffishness. They were willing to accept me as just another student on campus. They were willing to develop their own opinions.

On the same day that the football player asked me to the fraternity party, another freshman, whom I met in the hall prior to an orientation meeting, asked to sit with me during the session. Inside, he introduced me to several of his friends. Suddenly I was feeling like the most popular girl on campus.

Not only were they nice, friendly people, but they expressed a genuine interest in me. They wanted to hear my opinions on topics they were discussing. In the days to come, I found myself smiling more than I ever had in my life. There were times when I all but forgot about the home restrictions that still ruled my existence.

For the first time in my life I was even gaining some insight into people. In my first week on campus I happened to see a boy I had attended high school with; I spoke to him. He acted as if he hadn't even heard me—which wasn't all that surprising in view of the fact that he had not said a word to me in our four years in high school. Some time later, however, he saw me with a group of his own friends and came up, put his arm around me in a friendly gesture, and made a rather elaborate production of our having attended the same school. "Pam and I," he said, "have been friends for a long time." Which, of course, was an out-and-out lie. He had simply seen that I was accepted by the others and was using me to further his own cause, whatever it might have been.

Hypocrisy, I immediately decided, was something I needed no part of. Later, after the others had left, I approached him and said, "Maybe you can explain to me why, since we were such close friends in high school, you never said a word to me in four years."

He was obviously embarrassed and offered a meek apology. "You always seemed so shy back then that I never knew what to say to you," he said.

I smiled. " 'Hello' would have been nice."

For those first few weeks of college, I was happier than I had ever been. I enjoyed the college atmosphere, and I was finally making new friends among people my own age. But I seemed to be living two lives.

Though I was a college student, paying my own way, I was still living at home, subject to the same rules I'd grown up with. If someone wanted to take me to a movie, he first had to meet my father. If he wanted to talk with me on the phone in the evening he had to be prepared to limit the call to five minutes.

Once, on a double date with a group of newfound friends whose company I enjoyed very much, it was collectively decided after the movies that we should stop for a pizza. I had to bow out—I was due home in fifteen minutes. I'll never forget the stunned looks everyone gave me. They simply could not believe that a college freshman had to be in by 10:30 P.M. or not be allowed to go out again for two weeks.

In time, word got around about the strict social boundaries I had to stay within. And as the word spread, the calls and offers to go out slowed dramatically, then stopped. Once again my parents had won their quiet battle to keep me from venturing into a world they did not embrace.

And once again I found myself retreating into my shell. The groups I had briefly been a part of gradually slipped away, to enjoy their own fun, free from the childhood restrictions that were still so much a part of my life. Too quick to resign myself to the fate I felt was mine, I focused my efforts on my studies and my work.

My tentative but encouraging steps forward came to a

halt. I had only just begun to learn some valuable lessons: to warm to the approach of others, to feel comfortable in personal dealings with them. But there were other lessons—even more valuable ones—yet to be learned. Still shy and lacking confidence, I was unable to initiate a relationship; if another person accepted me first, then I could respond with warmth and a smile. And social situations remained to be conquered: In a small, informal gathering I felt relaxed and accepted, but a party with a lot of strangers was still a frightening experience that sent me back to my wallflower days.

I like to think that I might have overcome those fears and self-doubts under more normal circumstances. But, offered no encouragement in that area at home, tightly bound to the demands of my parents, I gave up any real attempt to overcome the problems before I truly began.

If I was to be allowed any kind of social life at all, I soon realized, it was to be with Ernest. Parental restrictions and rules and frowns of disfavor disappeared any time he came around. We continued to date and not once did he ever express any concern about my father's domination over my life. It even occurred to me that Ernest viewed it as normal and acceptable.

When I enrolled in college, it was my ambition to major in psychology and advertising, but soon Ernest had joined forces with my parents in trying to convince me that neither major held promise of a stable profession once I had earned my degree. I should, they all insisted work toward becoming an elementary-school teacher.

Never stopping to consider that I was old enough to do my own thinking, I changed my major. Everyone was happy with the decision—except me.

Not that I didn't like children. On the contrary, I had enjoyed being around young kids all my life. But while I said nothing about it to anyone, I was convinced that my personality was hardly suited to a successful teaching career. I was a nervous type and too wrapped up in my own multitude of problems to be able to work with a classroom of youngsters.

But Ernest said, "Teaching is one of the most stable professions. You can always get a job as a teacher. If something were to happen to me, you could be assured of finding a job."

On the basis of that short conversation, I made two major decisions: first, the one to change my course of study; second, I agreed to marry Ernest.

Again, I found myself doing what everyone else wanted me to do. I would work toward becoming a teacher. I would marry at the end of my sophomore year.

And I wondered if I would ever learn to be my own person.

4

The first few years of our marriage were fairly typical of the experience of young couples who are trying to combine school and work and make financial ends meet as best they can. Ernest was involved in a demanding orthodontics apprentice program and I was attending classes during the day, then rushing home to clean house and cook dinner. In the evenings and on weekends, I sold shoes.

The truth of the matter was we were both too busy even to get in each other's way. We did little more than meet, coming and going. Consequently, we got along pretty well. But we didn't get to know much about each other. At times it seemed we were just sharing the $97.50-per-month apartment we had moved into. We were more like college roommates than Mr. and Mrs.

I was certain that things, would be better once Ernest was able to set up his practice and I finished school and began teaching.

Immediately following graduation I got a job teaching fourth-graders in one of Dallas's more affluent schools. In time, the only reward I felt from my job came on those days when I would return to the apartment with my paycheck, endorse it, and hand it over to my husband.

Walking into that school every day was like going to jail. Though I liked children, I had no real concept of how to discipline them—and they picked up on that immediately. One afternoon, I remember, the principal stopped by, called me into the hall, and pointed out that the custodian had picked up more than fifty paper airplanes which had been sailed from the second-floor window of my classroom. I think he mentioned something about its setting a school record.

Still, the children seemed to enjoy my classes. They liked me and I liked them. It was the attitude of the other teachers that caused me the greatest discomfort.

Most of my colleagues were considerably older than I was and had stubbornly held to the traditional, old-school form of teaching. Students stayed at their desks, read a certain number of pages, then were tested. Punishment for any form of misbehavior was dealt swiftly and with great regularity.

In school I had been taught a more informal approach. We sang songs, took field trips, held discussions of various topics, and had far fewer tests. I disciplined my students only as a last resort. And then, I'm afraid, not very effectively. I just felt it was more important to teach than to punish and to praise, when deserved, rather than criticize. (In fact, I was told on more than one occasion that I had been graded exceptionally high on my student teaching while still in college because of my eagerness to get involved with the students.)

What I was trying to do as a teacher was to bring some degree of creativity and innovation to my job. While I felt I was getting positive results, I was viewed by my fellow teachers as a rebellious threat. They simply could not accept the fact that a learning experience could be fun and valuable to the students.

In time I began to hear the complaints. Students had begun to ask other teachers why they would not allow field trips, why they would not let the class go outside like Mrs. Lontos, why they didn't like singing songs. Needless to say, I wasn't the most welcome person in the teachers' lounge during breaks.

Eventually the pressures began to build and the criticism of my methods became less subtle. I had chosen to ignore the offhand remarks I'd heard from other teachers, feeling I was doing my job the best way I knew how. Then, however, the ultimatums began, in the form of memos from the principal: "You are not allowed to take the children out of the building during regular classroom periods." "Papier-mâché will no longer be allowed in the classrooms." "No pets, such as hamsters, will be allowed in the classrooms." "No more than two field trips per semester will be permitted any class." You get the idea. Since there was no hamster in any other classroom in school, since no other teacher allowed the students to work with papier-mâché, and few ever even considered a field trip, it was pretty clear for whom the directives were written. Shoot, I was causing the rule book to be completely rewritten.

And I kept them busy doing it. Early in my teaching career I would order an educational film weekly and show it to the children. Soon, that too was vetoed. I felt as if I were running into a brick wall at every turn. The school, it seemed to me, was doing everything in its power to make sure the learning process would be uninteresting, joyless, and anything but memorable—exactly the opposite of what I had been trained to do as a teacher in college.

Though the children liked me, my peers made it clear they had little use for my modern-day innovations. I was clearly the staff outcast, and in time it began to effect my enthusiasm.

There I was, doing something I had never really wanted

to do in the first place, trying to be as conscientious as I knew how, and it wasn't working. The high marks I had made in college obviously hadn't meant anything. Neither, for that matter, did the fact that the students seemed to enjoy my methods and learn from them, and that their parents regularly remarked on the enthusiasm their children displayed for what we were doing in class.

Psychological studies today show that people remember approximately 10 percent of what they hear, 20 percent of what they see, and 90 percent of what they participate in. Those figures didn't seem to register on my fellow educators.

The whole experience became a thoroughly miserable one. And, true to form, I began to wonder if maybe it wasn't all my fault. Perhaps I was wrong; maybe the extra effort I had brought to my work was counterproductive. I made up my mind that I was, in fact, a poor teacher. Had I been a more confident person, I might have thought my situation through and come to the proper conclusion that I was doing a good job. Instead, I automatically assumed that I must be wrong.

So, I decided to fight my battles quietly in the lunchroom. If it had been an average day, I would have one piece of chocolate cake with my meal. If things had really gone badly, I had two. The more isolated I felt from the other teachers, the more I ate. I really showed them. I went from a size six to a size sixteen, gaining sixty pounds. You can imagine how that looked on a person who was just five four and a half.

Now, on top of everything else, I was fat.

More and more, I found myself looking forward to the end of the day, when I could escape. In just a few hours, I would think, I can go to my shoe-selling job. There I would hear no criticism. Selling, I knew, was something I did well. The commissions I earned were tangible proof that I had some worth.

*   *   *

44

Things weren't exactly Camelot at home, either. Even when Ernest opened his practice, things went slowly for him. He had few patients and was obviously frustrated. There was little I could do to help him except to listen as he sat at the dinner table each evening withdrawn and distant.

On the other hand, when I mentioned the difficulties I was having at school he would make it clear that he wasn't interested. It was one of those "I've got problems of my own; don't dump yours on me" kind of responses.

Finally, I summoned the strength to make a decision about my situation. If I was a galloping failure as a teacher, well, I had never wanted to be one in the first place. I decided to go back to college for a master's degree in the subjects I had originally intended to pursue—psychology and advertising.

So I added to my list of activities. I continued teaching, maintained our home, sold shoes on Thursday nights and weekends, and went to night classes at SMU twice a week. I began to feel as if I were running a marathon that never ended. Quite often I would be up until three or four in the morning studying for an exam, then would sleep an hour or two before getting ready to teach all day.

I began to feel that I was running everywhere and getting nowhere. I was on a desperate search for something and I didn't even know what it was.

Compounding the situation was the fact that marriage had not provided the comforting stability I had hoped it would. And, in the first three years of marriage I had not become pregnant. Perhaps a family—a child of our own—would bring some solidity to our relationship and give me the purpose in life that I felt I badly needed.

When another year had passed without any indication that we were going to have a child of our own, we decided to look into the possibility of adopting. The idea filled me with a new enthusiasm for life. Suddenly the long work hours, the studying, and the financial problems did not weigh on me so heavily. I had something to look forward to. In time, I had been assured by the adoption agency, I would be a mother.

That, I felt, would finally add the much-needed new meaning to my life.

Long before the call came advising us that our little girl was waiting, I spent a great deal of time thinking how it would be to have a baby. My life would surely change, taking a new direction which, I felt, would lead to happiness and fulfillment.

It was midmorning when I was summoned to the principal's office for the call I had been waiting for. "We have your baby," the voice on the phone said, "and you can pick her up this afternoon." I first called my husband to tell him the good news, then immediately advised the principal that I would no longer be able to teach. I was going to be a mother to my own child instead of trying to educate the children of others.

I then returned to my classroom and told the news to my students. They received it with mixed emotions. They were excited that I was to have a baby but seemed genuinely disappointed that I would no longer be their teacher. Both reactions made me feel better than I had about myself in some time. I promised to bring the baby in to meet them.

That afternoon I saw the most wonderful sight I'd ever seen. She was twelve days old, healthy, and beautiful. We had already decided on her name: Anna-Marie.

There is, of course, a great difference between adoption and having your own child. The nine-month biological changes, the mental preparation for the baby's arrival, the morning sickness, the back pains, trips to the doctor, and finally being wheeled into the delivery room—all these are not a part of the adoption process. Instead, you do a lot of paperwork, praying, and waiting. Then, suddenly, you're an instant parent.

There's a wonder about it all the same. The love and

excitement are there. But if you've had a child of your own, just consider this: You get up one morning, feeling fine; you go off to work like any other day; then suddenly you get a call to be there at 2:00 P.M. and pick up your new child.

One night you're sleeping in a noiseless apartment with no life other than that of the two adult inhabitants. The following night you're up and down, feeding the new member of the family, changing diapers, worrying about things you have never had cause to worry about before.

The agency had assured us the adoption process would be long, and wearisome. They had repeatedly advised us not to get our hopes up immediately. Patience, they said, was the order of the day. Try not even to think about getting a child for at least a year or two. Maybe even longer. Which is what we did. Neither Ernest nor I had even begun to make serious plans for Anna-Marie's arrival when we received the call that we could pick her up. Needless to say, we did a lot of hurry-up shopping that afternoon.

Still, I could not have been happier. Ernest, too, seemed genuinely delighted. I was certain this was the new beginning we had both been looking for.

When we brought the baby home, my father was there almost immediately to meet his granddaughter. I don't recall ever seeing him so excited. "I'm going to come over every day," he told me. "I want to be able to watch her grow up. She's wonderful."

This small, fragile, ever-so-innocent child, less than two weeks old, seemed to have the power to bring us all together and I loved her even more for it.

It was because of her that we began discussing plans to move out of our tiny apartment and purchase a small house. Ernest's business was picking up, we'd saved some of the money I had earned, and we decided that if we really watched our pennies we could afford it. Dad offered to help decorate the house once we moved in.

With the baby, the new family feeling, and the excitement of getting a house, I found myself thinking more positively than I had in some time. I was feeling good about myself and my future—our future. In just a couple of months I would have the master's degree I'd worked so hard for, I would have my house and my baby. I began to believe I had finally emerged from that long, dark tunnel which had all but suffocated me for so many years.

As it turned out, there was an oncoming train at the end of that tunnel.

One Sunday afternoon, as we were packing to move into our new house, I received the news that my father had suffered a stroke and heart attack and had died, at the age of fifty-four. I simply could not accept it. All my life I had tried as hard as I knew how to please him, to win his praise. And finally, just as I felt I had earned his blessings, everything ended. I had proven myself to him by making good grades, by earning a living not only for Ernest and me but also being able to help him financially from time to time even after I left home. He was pleased at having a granddaughter and was looking forward to my getting my master's. Until the moment I learned of his death, I had not realized how important he had been to me. Earning his approval had, I realized, been one of the major motivating forces in my life.

Despite the difficulties we'd had, I considered him my best friend. After I was married he would come by regularly, to talk and lend encouragement in his own way. I think probably I was the only person who knew just how unhappy he was with his own life and I sympathized with him. We had long talks that made both of us feel better. I had looked forward to having him in the audience at my graduation ceremonies, and envisioned his shedding a proud tear as I became the first member of the family ever to receive a master's degree.

That spring I did get my degree. My husband expressed no interest in attending my graduation ceremonies. My mother called just hours before my final exam and urged me not to take it, to forget the idea of getting a degree I had no use for. And since my father was no longer alive to be there, I decided not even to go myself. It depressed me greatly to realize there was no one interested in the two-and-a-half-year struggle I'd just put myself through. I had earned my master's but it had proved a hollow triumph.

For months after my father's death I thought of him often. It depressed me that he was not there when Anna-Marie took her first steps or said her first words. He never saw the home we moved into the day after his funeral. I missed him desperately. And for all his faults, his unreasonable demands, his unbending rules, the loans that were never repaid, and the criticisms he had directed at the few ambitions I had, I loved him in a way I've never loved anyone else in my life. He was my father. He was my friend. And he was gone.

As I look back on it, I think perhaps my father's death was more difficult for me to cope with because it came at a point in my life when I was riding a newfound emotional high. I had never been so optimistic, so confident that things were going to get better than they'd ever been. Had he died at a time when I was down, I might have accepted his passing more willingly. Not that I wouldn't have been just as sad, and missed him just as much. But when your frame of mind is such that you expect the worst, you might well be better prepared for a major loss.

All the wonderful plans now seemed useless. My optimism turned to a deep, black depression like none I'd ever experienced before.

I climbed into bed and didn't get out for five years.

5

There is a story, which I think of often, about a military family transferred to a base where housing was at a premium. Upon their arrival they checked into a motel while they looked everywhere in the immediate area of the base for a place to live, a house or an apartment—with no success. The situation began to seem hopeless, but there was never a hint of a suggestion that the wife and children should return to the home they had moved from, halfway across the United States. They were a family and they were going to stay together, whatever the housing problem.

Finally, after a couple of weeks of fruitless searching, the mother proposed a solution: "I spoke with the motel manager today," she said, over a dinner of fast-food hamburgers, "and he told me that he has one large unit that has a kitchen. He's willing to rent it to us. It's small, but we'll make it work. I arranged to help him with some of the daily cleaning chores here in exchange for a lower weekly rate on the room. This motel will be our new home."

There was considerable discussion of the inconveniences that were certain to arise in such cramped quarters, but everyone was in agreement with the mother's plan. If that was what was necessary to keep the family together, everyone would pitch in and do his best to make it work.

Soon, school started and the children, adapting to new surroundings as only kids can, made new friends and occasionally brought them to the motel to visit in the afternoons.

One young visitor, the daughter of an officer on the base, was visibly concerned that her new friend was having to live in a motel rather than a more comfortable and spacious house. As they sat on the steps leading to the motel room, the youngster said, "I'm sorry you don't have a home."

Her friend smiled, shrugged her shoulders, and said, "It's okay. We have a home. It's just that we don't have a house to put it in right now."

My situation was just the opposite. I finally had a house to call my own and a family to live in it. But it was not a home. I quickly realized that there were ingredients far more important to the making of a home than furniture, brightly colored kitchen curtains, and a two-car garage. Even Anna-Marie's delightful presence couldn't make it into what I had fantasized it would be.

What we had was a house that we simply were not able to turn into a home.

It was a state of affairs I could not understand. My husband's practice had begun to improve dramatically and for the first time in my adult life I was neither working nor attending classes. I had long dreamed of the luxury of devoting all my energies to being a wife and mother. I now awakened to the reality of the most depressing time I've ever experienced.

As one with a great deal of energy, I found that I ran out of things to do at home by midday. Anna-Marie was still sleeping a good deal of the time, so I found myself spending hours reading, watching television, and waiting for my husband to come home. Restlessness began to gnaw at me, growing daily. I had no idea how to control it or compensate for it. You can, after all, rearrange furniture and dust just so many times.

Ernest, meanwhile, seemed very comfortable with our new life. A quiet, passive man, he would return home, play with the baby for a while, have dinner, then settle in to read the paper or watch television. If I suggested hiring a babysitter and going out to a nice restaurant for dinner he made it clear that such an outing would be a needless extravagance. My high level of energy bothered him. He could not understand why I couldn't be content to spend a quiet evening in silence, mesmerized by TV or a book.

We simply didn't talk. If I tried to express my frustrations, he tuned me out. More than once he walked away from me as I was in mid-sentence. Clearly, his was an I-don't-bring-my-problems-to-you; you-don't-bring-yours-to-me attitude.

In retrospect, I can see that I should have been angered. Instead, I viewed my husband's attitude as a mirror of his strength. He was, I felt, a person of great self-control, one who was not bothered by anything. On the other hand, I began to look at my own problems as a weakness. My inability to cope indicated to me that I was a negative force in Ernest's life: I was not a good wife; my problems were a hindrance to a promising young doctor on the rise. My self-worth took yet another nose dive.

In the face of Ernest's lack of response to my aggressive approach to conversation, I tried another tack. I withdrew, bound my feelings tightly, and became even more passive than he was. I no longer expressed opinions, offered no suggestions. I spoke only when spoken to.

And it worked. Ernest seemed far more willing to talk

to me when I was "down." In a bizarre, tremendously unhealthy way, I was rewarded with occasional bits of attention. And I became more and more miserable with each passing day.

Yet the idea of divorce or separation never entered my mind. The fault, I was convinced, was mine. I was too impulsive, too demanding, too much of a chatterbox. I came to the conclusion that I did not deserve a husband who was so self-assured, so confident and secure.

The next downward step was to decide that I was equally unfit as a mother.

Stranded in a house and a way of life that offered me little joy and no self-respect, I began toying with the idea of suicide. Maybe, I thought, the biggest favor I could do my husband and child would be to remove myself from their lives.

I thought about it often, but lacked the courage to carry out any plan. Instead, I continued in a state of limbo, going nowhere, doing nothing, stepping constantly backward into a dark depression that closed in around me, suffocating me as if I were living my life in an airless room.

Sleep became my only escape.

When Anna-Marie was in bed, sleeping, so was I. When she awoke, I would take her to her playpen, then stretch out on the couch nearby and sleep some more. When it came time to prepare dinner, I would get up, cook, then return to bed. Chores like cleaning the house and shopping were accomplished in the briefest possible time and with the least expenditure of energy.

For a while I had hired a babysitter on occasion so that I might get away from the house for a few hours to go shopping or have lunch somewhere. Now I continued the practice of hiring a babysitter, but I never left the house. With someone there to look after my daughter, I could retreat to my bedroom and sleep.

I began to resemble one of those horrid late-show zombies. My routine: Sleep until midmorning; get up and take care of the baby; then wait for the sitter to arrive in the afternoon so I could go back to bed; get up to fix dinner for my husband and prepare Anna-Marie for bed; then retire again.

There were many days when I slept for more than twenty hours.

The complete absence of physical activity resulted in another complication. Though I wasn't really eating that much, I began to gain weight again. And the more I gained, the deeper my depression grew. I had finally quit weighing when I reached 160 pounds and could not get into most of my clothes. I never knew my top weight and back then I didn't even want to know!

Occasionally there were days when I realized the fix I was in and made up my mind to get up, get dressed, and begin rearranging my life. I knew I needed to get out, to become active again, to return to the living. But my best intentions were weighed down by lack of energy. It was as if something were pressing down on me, driving me back to bed—back to my place.

The time came when I could not even muster the strength to leave the bed when I was hungry. Desperate about a situation I really did not understand, I called a doctor, hoping he might provide me some reason for my lack of energy. After a physical examination he informed me that the only problem he could determine was that I was overweight. He suggested a diet, some vitamins, and physical activity.

Obviously, my problem was not one that X rays or physical exams were going to reveal. I thanked him and went home—and back to bed.

On several occasions after we adopted Anna-Marie, Ernest and I had discussed the possibility of a second child. It would be nice, we thought, if our daughter had a younger brother or sister to grow up with. We talked with the adoption agency, seeking their advice about how soon we should apply for a second child.

The procedure, we were told, would take several years—maybe as many as five—so if we were certain we wanted to add to our family, we should make application immediately. At the time I was feeling better and agreed that we should go ahead. Surely in four or five years I would have my life in order and be ready to accept the responsibility of a second child. And, too, there was the chance that the addition of another person to the family might cause some magical revival in our relationship.

I was in bed asleep—as usual—when only four months later the call came one morning from the adoption agency. Through my fog I heard a cheerful voice: "We've got your little boy."

Since the caller, in her excitement, had not identified herself, I didn't understand what she was trying to say. I told her I didn't have a little boy. She laughed, explained herself, then said, "You do now."

I was stunned. Anna-Marie was nearing two and a half, I was in such a depressed state that the doctor whom I had visited earlier was calling daily just to make sure I had not summoned the courage to take my own life, and now I was just a short car ride from having another baby to take care of.

The process, the adoption official explained, had been speeded up because the little boy was, as she put it, "a perfect match" for us. Lamely, I said I had been under the impression that the procedure could take as long as five years.

"Well," she said, "you just got lucky. You're going to love him. He's fair-skinned, blue-eyed, and blond."

I called my husband to tell him the news, then set about readying myself to meet my new son. Ryan is now twelve years old and, like Anna-Marie, one of the true joys of my life. On that day, however, I could do nothing but wonder how in the world I was going to care for another child when I wasn't able even to take care of myself.

When we arrived at the adoption home, everything was already moving at full speed. The paper work had begun and one of the nurses hurried my daughter off to see her new baby brother.

In a matter of minutes they returned and placed a beautiful sixteen-day-old boy in my arms. We were given his birth certificate, some background information, and in no more than fifteen minutes were on our way home.

The tears I shed as we drove home with the newest member of our family should have been tears of joy. In truth, however, they were not.

In short order I reached a new low. If I had entertained any will to climb out of my depression, it disappeared. I gave up totally. And in giving up I found it easier to cope. I could manage, with some effort, the basic functions necessary to take care of the children, but that was all. I left it to others to take care of me. My doctor, finally determining that I was suffering from some form of chemical imbalance, prescribed antidepressants. Neither his diagnosis nor his prescription did any good.

Any ambition I might once have had disappeared. I felt totally worthless, unable even to think about personal achievement. My world continued to shrink. The college degree I had worked so hard for meant nothing. The experience I had gained while working no longer offered me any sense of self-worth. I was drowning in a sea of negative thinking, ready to quit before ever really starting.

While I was still working on my master's degree at night at SMU, one of my psychology teachers had called me into his office after class one evening and begun asking me questions about myself. Where did I live? Where had I gone to high school? Where had I worked? Had I ever done any traveling?

I had no idea what he was getting at as I answered his questions. Finally he shook his head in amazement. "What you're telling me," he said, "is hard to believe. You're almost thirty years old and your entire radius of experience is within a two-mile area. In this day and time, that is inconceivable."

Now, however, that radius had narrowed even more. I rarely left home. I didn't want to see anyone, to risk the dangers of conversation or having anyone see that I had grown into an overweight, depressed housewife. I was more comfortable locking myself into my own residential prison.

And it was there that I found myself contemplating suicide more and more seriously as each day passed. Not only was I making little or no contribution to anything or anyone, but I had become a handicap to those around me. I was nothing more than a burden. Maybe, I found myself thinking, I would be doing my husband and children a favor by removing myself from their way.

It was a thought that consumed me for several years. But—thank God—I had neither the strength nor the courage to put the thought to action.

6

Though I have never been attracted to liquor, I have a strong feeling of kinship with the millions of recovering alcoholics in the country today. Time and again I have heard their stories: how they had to reach the very bottom, often losing family, career, and all self-respect, before being able to summon the courage and strength to begin the climb back.

Though it was depression, not alcohol, that had taken command of my life, my problems were similar. I had lost all self-respect and hadn't the slightest degree of confidence that I would ever be able to redirect my life positively. I violently disliked the person I had become. I felt alone, unloved, and absolutely useless.

Which is to say I, too, had finally reached bottom. How I came to realize that, I honestly can't say. I had no yardstick by which to measure the ultimate degrees of depression or self-pity. Nor did I have any timetable for despair. I simply realized one morning as I lay in bed that things had deteriorated to a point where I did not wish to live another day in such an atmosphere.

Neither, I decided, did I want to take my own life.

That decision left me with only one course of action: I was going to have to do something to set my own house in order. I had spent my entire life waiting for someone else to do it for me, and no knight on a white charger had miraculously appeared. The calvary, I determined, was not going to come charging to my rescue.

The only person, they say, who can really give an alcoholic the will to improve and overcome his illness is the alcoholic himself. Oh, there are those who can lend support along the way, once the decision to recover has been made, but that first step is up to the individual needing the help. Certain forms of depression have much the same requirement.

I decided, then, to make a concerted effort to find my way out of the black hole that had become my habitat. Though I didn't realize it at the time, I was bone-weary of paying the high price of failure. I didn't go so far as to entertain grand fantasies of overnight personality reversal, but I made up my mind that I was going to find a better way of living—if it killed me.

I decided my first step back into the real world would be in the direction of a neighborhood health club. There, I hoped to begin losing some of the weight I had been putting on since the chocolate-cake lunches of my teaching career.

If I could get my weight down, I figured, I would feel better about the way I looked. And if I could accomplish that, maybe the next step—whatever it was to be—would be easier.

If one can be determined without confidence, I was. I knew my goal, though I wasn't at all sure I could reach it.

But I had made up my mind at least to try. For me, that was a major decision.

For the first time in longer than I cared to remember, the focus of my attention turned to me. I like to think it wasn't a selfish, vain concern. Rather, it occurred to me that if my life was to change, I would have to be the one to change it. If I was to enjoy any measure of happiness, I was going to have to seek it. I was going to have to take responsibility for myself.

Needless to say, I didn't exactly bound through the doors of the health club, grandly announcing that I was going to tone up, firm up, and take on the world. I was hesitant, skeptical, hoping for a miracle but not at all sure one was possible.

The owner of the club, a man named Jim, strongly believed in what he was trying to help people accomplish at his club. A former collegiate football player, now in his mid-twenties, he was the picture of fitness himself. He approached me with an energy and enthusiasm I had rarely encountered. While I was pessimistic, he was assuring me that I could get rid of my excess weight. Frankly, he sounded like someone badly wanting to sell a membership. And I was an easy sale.

Those first few days of exercise were torturous. Every muscle in my body was telling me the whole idea was foolish. The pain, however, was a welcome signal: If it was hurting that much, it had to be doing me some good. I began to feel a tentative optimism, and even a sort of pride in my sore and aching muscles. Though it was pain I was feeling, to feel anything was a step in a new direction for me.

So there I was, taking it one day at a time, but still not really knowing how long I would stick with it before giving up and returning to my bed and zombielike existence. Jim, who had seen my kind before, had no trouble recognizing my lack of confidence.

One afternoon as I was leaving the club he stopped me. He began by praising the progress I was making. I had lost a couple of pounds but not enough to indicate that I was really getting anywhere. But for several mintues he talked of the distance I had come in a short period of time. "The trick now," he said, "is to stay with it. Motivation is the key to getting where you want to be. I can show you the exercises and give you advice on what to eat and not to eat, but all the work is up to you. You've got to say motivated.

"Quite frankly, I don't think there's anyone in this club who seems to be as miserable as you. I haven't seen a smile from you since you walked through that door. I'll be honest with you: You have a long way to go. But you can get there—if you'll stay with it."

He handed me a set of motivational tapes. "These have helped me," he said. "I'd like to lend them to you. Listen to them when you get home."

That evening, lying in bed with every muscle in my body aching, I heard the voice of Zig Ziglar for the first time. The tapes were titled "How to Stay Motivated," and they seemed to have been made with me in mind.

Though I wasn't aware of it at the time, I had taken another step in the right direction. What Ziglar was saying intrigued me: People, he said, are constantly making decisions to do something, only to find it difficult to make the commitment necessary to the success of the resolve. Your success or failure is the by-product of that commitment or lack thereof.

For instance, it is really not that difficult to make up your mind to lose weight, then actually take it off. But without the proper commitment, you will eventually regain those pounds. That's why you see so many people whose weight goes up and down like a yo-yo. They've never fully committed themselves to achieving their goal. Until you realize that you're into a long-range, day-in, day-out effort, you aren't going to be the success you can be.

I listened to those tapes over and over—probably fifty times. And every time I heard them they made more sense. Then I sought out books on motivation and tapes by others I thought might help me. I suddenly had a strong thirst for knowledge in the field of self-help and was pleased to discover there was good, sound advice to be found.

Some will say I was looking for a crutch to lean on in times of low self-esteem and little confidence. I will give them absolutely no argument. I did need a crutch. I needed help and was not finding it anywhere else. Those tapes and books provided it. They helped me to start thinking about the importance of making a commitment.

When I felt bad, down—which was most of the time—I forced myself to listen to the tapes and read the books, hoping to get myself into a more positive frame of mind. On those occasions when I did feel good, I read and listened in an attempt to stay that way. I don't think I fully realized it then, but for the first time in my life I had, in truth, made a commitment.

In time the physical workouts weren't as agonizing. In fact, I began to look forward to them. Exercise, I came to realize, had a cleansing, exhilarating effect on me. The tiredness I felt at the end of each day's session had become a reward of sorts, giving me a sense of accomplishment. I was losing weight and feeling better, physically and emotionally. I was, quite literally, coming back to life.

The next step, I decided, was to go back to work. For years I had thought about it occasionally, but each time had convinced myself I had no talents that were marketable other than teaching and selling shoes. The prospect of returning to either one of those occupations excited me not at all. I had no secretarial skills, so that line of work was out. Then too, when I did suggest that I might go back to work, my husband would make it immediately clear that it was an idea he scarcely welcomed. I was convinced I would be lucky to get a position as a check-out clerk in a grocery store. Then, as my depression became an increasingly heavy burden, I forgot about the idea all together.

Now, though, I was considering it seriously, getting excited about the idea of earning my own way, of accomplishing something outside the home. Already in the back of my mind I was beginning to think of an avenue of escape from my marriage, which had been going downhill for years. The depression I had suffered through had never really concerned Ernest. Rather, he seemed to feel more comfortable with our relationship when I was at my lowest. Though the idea of divorce gave me great moral difficulties, I slowly began to realize that if I was to survive and rebuild my life, I would have to do it on my own. I did not think of separation at this time.

That, quite simply, meant finding a job. As I pondered the possibilities, I asked myself two questions: What might I be good at? And what would I enjoy?

The answer to both questions was the same: sales.

The next step, obviously, was to determine where to go in search of a job. For some time my exposure to the outside world had been pretty limited. I had really ventured no farther than the health club. So, it was there that I went looking for a job. Selling memberships was a vital part of the operation, and it occurred to me that I was something of a walking billboard, proof that the physical fitness program the club offered worked.

I approached Jim: "You're the guy who got me off my rear end and into this program. You're the one who gave me the tapes and got me motivated to do something with my life. Now, you have to hire me!" (I'm afraid that looks far more self-assured in print than it sounded. Actually, my tone was more desperate than demanding.)

When Jim did give me a job, I had no idea that I would receive a bonus which I can't, to this day, put a price tag on. His approach to business was based on positive thinking. In his view, nothing was impossible. *Can't* wasn't a part of his business vocabulary.

He chose to ignore the negative attitude I still had about myself. He carefully explained various sales techniques to me. In a gentle way he pressured me to extend myself, for my own good. I had the potential and the ability, he would say, so there was no reason I couldn't make sales.

Jim maintained an air of optimism that affected everyone around him. Several times a week he had his employees listen to the same motivational tapes he had loaned to me. We learned sales techniques and how best to create a positive image. From those sessions came an enthusiasm that was infectious. Everyone, the salespeople and the instructors, came away with new zest for the job.

It didn't take me long to get swept up in the feeling. While I was still regarded by others as a very shy, standoffish person, I had already come a long way. And with each passing day I was breaking new emotional ground.

I found quickly that I hadn't lost my touch for sales and soon was earning a salary that enabled me to buy myself some new (smaller) clothes, pay off some bills, and even put some money in savings.

And with each accomplishment, Jim challenged me to take an even bigger step the next time. One morning he suggested that I go into downtown Dallas and visit several banks to see if I could sell club memberships to some of the executives. I was game, but had to tell him I didn't think I could drive in the freeway traffic.

"What do you mean?" he asked. "You can drive, can't you?"

"Yes," I answered, "but I've never tried to drive downtown." It was embarrassing to admit that I had lived in Dallas all my life, was thirty years old, yet feared the very idea of trying to get onto one of the local freeways and find my way downtown.

"Come on," he said, almost dragging me out of the club and into the parking lot. He told me to get behind the wheel and then began giving me directions. In short order we were on the freeway, and I knew exactly how demolition-derby entrants must feel. But we made it downtown, found a parking lot, and walked to a restaurant.

"Look," Jim said to me, "you have a tremendous amount of ability. You're intelligent, nice-looking—you've got everything in the world to make it big. What's the matter with you?"

I did not bore him with the details of my five-year bout with depression or the problems I was dealing with in my marriage. And he did not press the matter further. I don't think he really expected an answer to his question. He was simply trying to make a point. It was his way of taking me by the shoulders, shaking me, and telling me to wake up to the possibilities around me.

In time, I was whizzing all over Dallas, selling memberships faster than anyone on the sales staff. It was as if a whole new world had opened to me. I didn't have the polish of some of the other salespeople, nor was my technique the best—but I was improving every day. My confidence began to feed on itself. I actually expected to make a sale, even before introducing myself to a prospective member. I sold to bank presidents, people I met coming out of Safeway, ladies I ran into in dress shops. I even went into a laundromat next to the club and found a bored gentleman waiting for his clothes to dry, offered him a tour of the facilities, and sold him a membership.

In a relatively short period of time I had come a very long way.

Jim shared a philosophy with me for which I shall forever be indebted to him: "Don't," he told me repeatedly, "say you can't do something until you've tried!"

One morning, just as I reported to work, he approached me with a new challenge. "We need some radio ads," he said. "Think you can write some thirty-second radio commercials?"

I wasn't about to tell him he was talking to someone who wrote so poorly that she did posters of Einstein's theory of Relativity to get out of writing a term paper in college physics class; that I was a hopeless, fumbling dyslexic who had trouble even writing down a telephone number correctly. "I'll try," I said.

I struggled all day with those ads, trying to make them sound as if a professional had written them. Each one sounded worse than the last. Finally, I decided I would write the ads in the style I used for a personal sales pitch. Jim read them, said they sounded fine to him, and sent them off to the radio station.

The ads began running the following Monday morning. By the end of that day we had received one hundred calls instead of the customary three or four.

For the next year I was in charge of all the club's advertising. I had cleared another hurdle—and found myself racing toward a new and exciting career.

7

Generally, we tend to measure the value of a job by the size of the paycheck we receive. Money, quite frankly, has become the American way of keeping score, of determining how we are progressing toward our own goals and how we're measuring up against our competitors.

I'll not go so far as to call this a negative philosophy. Rather, I would suggest that money is one of the many motivating forces in society today. It would be narrow-minded, however, to view earning power as the be-all and end-all. When I began getting nice commission checks from the health club, I felt better about myself than I had in years. I was putting some money in savings, helping to pay the bills, didn't feel guilty about buying a new dress, and even financed a bank loan to buy myself a car.

But the money I was earning did a great deal more for me. In a sense it bought me a new attitude. The job put me in the company of a number of new people daily, removing me from the isolated existence I had been so long locked into. Out of necessity, I became more outgoing, learned to look people in the eye and to smile again. I made new friends who seemed to enjoy my company as much as I did theirs. I found that because of my ambition to succeed in business, I was finally succeeding in life.

I think back often and give thanks that I found something strong enough to pull me out of my shell. There's no way I will ever be able to put a dollar value on that, except to say it has been worth more to me than any amount of money I may ever make.

One of the greatest ironies I encountered as I became more and more involved in my work was that I found I was getting more done at home. Though I was putting in long hours on the job, I was also spending more time with my children than ever before, managing to keep the house looking nice, and even becoming more inventive in the kitchen. Though my new outlook did little to improve the long-standing problems between Ernest and me, I found myself better able to cope with them. While he obviously liked the contribution I was making to the family income, he was far from encouraging about my work. My ambition seemed to irritate him, and he wasn't interested in hearing about my new friends. So we just didn't talk much. He buried himself in his work and I continued to enjoy mine. At home, in the evenings, we were like strangers living in the same house.

The children, of course, sensed the tension and made it a point to avoid both of us when we were together. In time it was as if they had two families. While in the company of their father, without me, they seemed happy, carefree. The same held true when they were with me, out for a movie or dinner or a trip to the park.

I began to see their attitude toward me change. It was obvious they liked my new energy, my confidence, and the attention I was finally paying to them. They, too, became more outgoing, laughing more, talking to me about their problems. They seemed to develop more friendships at school, did better academically, and for the first time in their lives showed pride in their mother.

Yet things were far from picture perfect. Ernest and I drifted farther and farther apart. On the other hand, my life was generally so much better than it had been for such a long time that I found even my marital difficulties less depressing. I was directing my energies and concern in other directions and, in doing so, finding most of the hours of each day fulfilling and happy.

The marriage, I felt could not last much longer. Still, I hoped for some miracle to heal the wounds and bring us together as a family. Though I continued to think about it from time to time, the idea of leaving my husband filled me with overwhelming guilt and fear.

To avoid such thoughts, I worked even harder at my job, deciding to ignore the negatives and concentrate on something I did well. Maybe I hadn't been the ideal wife, hadn't even been able to have children, but I had found something I was good at: I could sell. And it was good for my self-image to close deals and rush back to the office with a purse filled with applications for new membership.

If I was to become the person I wanted to be—and, frankly, I still had no real idea who that was—I was going to have to focus on the positives and put the negatives aside. In the long run, all of us would be better off for it.

One of the most exciting things about ambition is that, once in full stride, it knows no bounds. No sooner is one goal reached than another is set. Motivation begins to feed on itself; momentum creates more momentum.

One day in 1977, I heard that a new radio station was going on the air in Dallas. In the year I had been handling advertising for the health club, I had come to know a number of station managers in the local market and I was fascinated by the electronic media. The power of radio and television amazed me. They could popularize a certain kind of music, make sales pitches, or inform the public far more quickly than the print media.

For some time I'd had in the back of my mind a lurking ambition to get into radio sales, but I simply hadn't the first idea how to make the transition. It occurred to me that no sales manager would be turning backflips over my experience, consisting of working in a women's shoe department and selling memberships to overweight women and out-of-shape executives.

But I decided there could be no harm in asking. After all, there were thirty-four radio stations in Dallas. It seemed unlikely that the newest one on the block was going to have too many high-powered salespeople beating down the door.

In that sense, I was wrong. When I spoke to the sales manager he told me that all sales positions had been filled. "I'm sorry," he said. "But I don't have a list to give you." What, I asked him, was a list? He explained that it was a list of prospective clients given to each salesperson.

"I've never worked from a list," I said. "I won't need one." (The first statement was true; the second, a guess.)

"Look," he went on. "I'd like to give you a chance. I think it would be nice to have an experienced salesperson like yourself selling ads for our station. But I couldn't afford another draw." (A "draw" is money advanced a salesman against his hoped-for commission. If his sales don't meet expectations for the month, he still has the draw to fall back on.)

"I've never worked on anything but commission," I told the sales manager. "I don't need a list and I don't need a draw. All I'm asking is the chance to try to sell ads for this station."

In truth the guy had nothing to lose. Without making the slightest commitment, he had the chance to add to his sales staff. If I sold one ad, he was ahead of the game. He shrugged his shoulders, smiled, and told me I had the job.

The station had been on the air all of ten days when I went to work. Of the dozen or so people I mentioned my new job to, not one had heard of radio station KMGC. Had I know better, I would probably have been worried.

It had never occurred to me that the response of a potential client was directly related to the size of listening audience a salesperson could brag about. Neither did it occur to me that the lists, which had been handed out to other members of the station sales force, included the names of just about every possible customer in the listening market. What that left me was undiscovered clients: small companies, with small ad budgets, that had never tried to sell their products through radio commercials before.

I beat the bushes from early morning until late in the afternoon, and rare was the day I didn't return to the station with several new advertising clients. They were small accounts, to be sure, but when added together they made a rather lucrative package for the station. And provided me with a nice commission.

After three weeks I was the leading salesperson on the staff—and still didn't have a list to operate from. But I had caught a glimpse of what was on those lists and been stunned to see that none of the major department stores or car dealers or grocery chains was listed. It made no sense to me that the station had predetermined its own "comfort zone," resigning itself to selling to medium-size advertisers, not even approaching the big ones.

Again flying on hope and blissful ignorance, I made up my mind to go after the big accounts. After all, no one else was, so I wasn't going to be stepping on anyone's toes.

I found out why we had avoided that area of sales when I made my first sales pitch. In fact, I hadn't even given my pitch before the advertising director, sitting behind a big desk in a big office, asked a question I had no answer for: "Where are you in the book?"

"What book?"

He had an amused look on his face by this time, obviously aware he was dealing with something less than a seasoned veteran. "The Arbitron, the book that lists all the radio stations by the number of listeners they have. People wanting to advertise want to know how many people they're going to be reading, right?"

"Right."

He pulled out his own copy of the Arbitron ratings, asked me the call letters of my station, and went in search of KMGC. After a minute he looked up and said, "You aren't even in here." It was as if he were telling me the station I worked for didn't even exist.

The reason we weren't listed, naturally, was because we were so new and didn't have enough listeners to make the rankings. Even if we had been listed, we would have been thirty-fourth in a field of thirty-four. Maybe, I thought, it was good that we weren't in The Book.

I left the man's office a little embarrassed. I also realized that if I was to sell to any of the major advertisers, I was going to have to develop a new approach, something that could overcome the newness of the station and the fewness of our listeners.

It was clear to me that the standard radio sales pitch—show them the format, the geographical coverage, a list of the music played, the ownership of the company, etc.—would not work. When selling health-club memberships, I had been told to be aggressive, to convince a potential member of his or her need for that membership. That technique, I decided, was what I would try on the people to whom I hoped to sell radio time. So what if we didn't have that many listeners? Those we did have were important, and they were potential car buyers. They would eventually need a new washing machine or power lawn mower. They were interested in the latest fashions and liked to shop at the grocery stores that offered the best buys.

I sold the quality of the station and the life-style of its

listeners, rather than the quantity. To car dealers who had refused even to see me, I pressed the point that surely they would not instruct one of *their* salesmen not even to talk to a customer. I pushed harder than I ever had in my limited sales life—and began to make small inroads. I made a couple of sales, got to talk with more people than I probably had any right to expect, and felt I was making progress.

Then I was called on the carpet. The sales manager, though pleased with the advertising revenue I had been generating in my few weeks on the job, suggested that others on the sales force had hinted I was a bit too aggressive in my approach, that I wasn't following the time-honored guidelines for selling radio commercials. "You've got to tone it down," he told me. "I appreciate your enthusiasm, but there are right and wrong ways to go about this business. We're low-keyed. We operate on the theory that we make the customer aware of what we have to offer, then leave it at that. When he's ready to buy, he'll call you."

My brief career as a radio-ad salesperson took a screaming nose dive. In my fourth week on the job I sold less advertising than I did in my first. I had thought broadcast sales was going to be exciting, fun, but I found myself ready to go back to the health club.

At lunch one day I told a friend of my decision, explaining that the challenge I had hoped to find just wasn't there. It was almost as if they were afraid to be aggressive. If, I said, they would let me sell ads the way I sold shoes and health-club memberships, it would really be fun—and I could make the station and myself a lot of money.

She looked at me for a minute, then said, "Why don't you just go back and do it that way?"

"Because they would probably fire me."

"So what? You're thinking about walking out anyhow. Try it your way, and see if you can convince them it will work. If it works out, fine. If not, go back to selling health-club memberships. You don't lose in either case. Do it that way and you'll never have to look back someday and ask yourself whether you might have been successful if you had tried it a different way."

It was the best pep talk I had ever heard. And it was what I had needed to hear.

For the next month I worked harder than I'd ever worked in my life. Using every sales technique I knew, I called on one potential client after another. I refused to take an immediate no for an answer. I assured those customers who turned me down that I would be back to see them. On the more positive side were several people who seemed genuinely surprised to see me. Surprised and, I thought, a little pleased.

As I became more comfortable with the sales formula I had devised, I began hearing fewer noes and enough yeses to assure me that my boss wasn't going to lecture me anymore on being too aggressive.

I had become acquainted with a number of salespeople from competing radio stations and found them always eager to talk about the business. Listening to them, I picked up tips that would help me improve my own presentation. In some cases I became comfortable enough with my competitors to ask some pretty personal business questions, like: how much did they generally average selling a month? The answer from large accounts was usually in the $60,000 to $70,000 range.

Suddenly one month, however, when I asked how much they had billed that particular month, most mentioned a figure in the neighborhood of $10,000. I was stunned. The month was just half over and I had already done triple that amount—and fully expected the figure to climb considerably before the month was out.

Again, I found I was the fortunate victim of ignorance about the business. I had asked the question in January! Historically, the month of January is considered a "dead" month in broadcast advertising. Coming on the heels of

Christmas buying, it is a time when advertisers see little benefit in buying radio time or newspaper space. For that reason, salespeople just coast through the month, not even calling on a number of their regular clients.

Unaware of the pattern, I had worked harder than ever at making sales—and in fact earned one of the largest commission checks ever written in radio sales in Dallas for that January. All because I didn't know it was supposed to be a bad month.

Which again proves that negative preconceptions can defeat you before you even start. A number of really fine salesmen, people considered among the best in the market, had blindly accepted as fact the long-standing myth that ads could not be sold in January. For a month every year they were defeated before they began—because they had already made up their minds that something was impossible.

From that month forward I was the top-grossing salesperson on our staff. In fact, on a monthly basis I was bringing in as much as the other six salespeople combined. Professionally, things were looking pretty good. Emotionally, I was feeling better about myself with each passing day, despite my recent decision to move from the house to an apartment. Our marriage had shown no sign of improvement. On the contrary. There were arguments in front of the children, followed by long spells of cold silence. I had reached a point in life where everything seemed reversed. Once, I had been so down on myself, so lacking in self-confidence, that I was certain the only person in the world who even tolerated my presence was my husband. Then, when I began to feel better about myself, an opposite reaction set in. My husband, it seemed, was the only one who didn't like the person I had become.

For a while, both of us felt bad about the separation. We both, I think, felt a certain degree of guilt. We talked about it occasionally, trying to determine where the responsibility, the fault, lay. We discussed the problems the separation and a possible divorce might cause for the children. We talked, but we resolved nothing.

In the midst of one of the severest ice storms in Dallas history, I fell walking out of the apartment and broke my leg. The doctors told me I would be in a cast for as long as six months. For the first time in quite a while, I allowed myself to feel down. Being immobile would make my job all but impossible. There was no way I could drive all over Dallas, making the calls I needed to make.

While I sat at home, feeling sorry for myself, Ernest came by. He asked me to come back home. He would take care of me. He would do everything he could to make our marriage work. We would get counseling. He would change. I cried a little and agreed to try it.

Things went smoothly until I began to weary of my depression and made up my mind to get back to work, one way or another, crutches or no crutches. The moment I began to show some assertiveness, things went back to the way they had been before the separation. Ernest wanted me down, passive, depressed.

A few years later I packed and left again, knowing I would never return. I left it all behind—money, house, furniture, everything but the children. I could *never* give them up. After a long battle, we decided on joint custody.

When most of your income is derived from outside sales— those made through calling on customers personally—near-immobilization can be a major blow. I considered my plight and devised a new plan of attack. I could still manage to get around enough to see some customers in person. I would call ahead to make sure an appointment was set for a specific time, then hobble my way into the office. My cast, in fact, became the best icebreaker I'd ever found. Clients were obviously impressed by my calling in person despite having to do so on crutches.

But I couldn't cover as much ground as before. So, I began doing some of my selling by telephone.

I'd never attempted phone sales before, feeling (as I still do) that personal contact is best. But when you can't get on with Plan A, go to Plan B.

My approach over the phone was basically the same as my personal one. I placed each call in a confident frame of mind, assuming even before dialing that I would make the sale. I made every effort to express that confidence in my voice. I was warm and friendly, but businesslike. Though I wasn't as effective as I might have been in person, my sales figures actually dropped very little.

It wasn't the way I preferred to sell—but the broken leg provided me an opportunity to explore an avenue I might never have ventured on otherwise. I found out I *could* do telephone sales. My canvas (or canvass?) was broadened. Something positive had been created from a negative situation.

Since the broken leg kept me in the office far more, I got to know the other sales personnel far better. We talked at great length about various sales techniques. I eagerly explained mine to them and told them about motivational tapes that I felt might benefit them. It pleased me that my ideas and suggestions were greeted with enthusiasm. In time, several others tried some of my techniques and their sales began to go up.

For the first time in my adult life I felt I was giving something to someone else—and that they appreciated it. There is a philosophy, which I've long believed in, that promises you will get everything you want out of life if only you are willing to help others achieve what they want as well.

Finally I was given the opportunity to test it—and I found it to be one hundred percent true.

8

I was really enjoying the management part of the business. It was fun to work with other salespeople, advising them, then watching as their billings climbed. In just a couple of months several of them had made jumps of from 300 to 500 percent. Everyone was excited, enthusiastic and optimistic.

Until the bottom fell out.

Suddenly our ratings, which hadn't been that healthy in the first place, began to fall. The small audience we had built in the year and a half the station had been on the air had managed to earn us a 2.6 rating in the Arbitron book. Now, bear in mind that a 2.6 is pretty low, even for a newly established station. The new ratings came out and we had dropped to 1.8 (1.8 of the people in the city listening to radio listened to KMGC).

There was a mad scramble for safety. The sales manager turned in his resignation almost immediately. Most of the sales staff left for jobs with other stations. The deejays were frantically searching for a station that had somebody listening.

And, of course, advertisers began canceling. The Book, as it is called in the broadcast business, was killing us. Which stunned me. I had never used The Book when I was selling. I was not intimidated by it and neither, for that matter, were my clients.

Making up my mind that there must be some opportunity in all this adversity, I went to the station manager. "Your sales manager has left and so have most of your experienced salespeople. Why don't you make me sales manager?"

He gave me a surprised look. I don't know whether he thought I was crazy for wanting the job or relieved that someone was committed to staying on and trying to put the station on its feet.

I explained to him that I would continue to sell in addition to handling the responsibilities of sales manager. I was pushing real hard for the job—a job no one in his right mind would have taken on a bet.

"Okay," he said, "let's give it a try. The job's yours." We shook hands.

I had just taken what might have been the absolute worst job in the United States and I was excited about it because I didn't know any better. I felt I had advanced, that I was appreciated, that I was needed.

What I didn't realize at the time was that I was putting my neck squarely on the chopping block. The corporate headquarters in Los Angeles would be watching the station carefully. If sales figures dropped, as they usually do after a ratings drop, the blame would fall squarely on the shoulders of the sales manager—me. I held my first sales meeting on the first day of September and wrote the figure $100,000 on the board. Around the room mouths literally dropped open.

I had been averaging between $30,000 and $40,000 in sales myself each month and felt the other three people on my staff could boost the total to the goal I had set. I spoke of techniques, promised motivational meetings, urged everyone to set sales goals, and generally gave what I felt was a pretty effective pep talk.

When the meeting was over the general manager called me to his office. "That was an excellent meeting," he said, "but I wonder if you have any idea what this station has been billing each month?"

I had no idea.

"We've been averaging in the neighborhood of forty-two thousand dollars. The truth of the matter is, your sales have been the bulk of our income. You've averaged around thirty-five thousand, and the others have made up the other seven thousand or so. What I'm saying is I'm afraid your goal for this month is a little unrealistic."

I went home that night and tossed and turned. I had assumed my own sales figures would drop, since I wouldn't be able to get out and sell as much as manager. The other three people, I had hoped, would take up the slack and help us to that $100,000 goal. For reasons I've never understood, things always look blackest in the middle of the night. It is the absolutely worst time to come to any kind of decision. But as I lay there, the station manager's words ringing in my ears, I decided to call a meeting the next morning and tell everyone I had reconsidered. I would drop the goal to $50,000.

The next day as I made the forty-five-minute drive to work, I listened to a motivational tape. By then I had become acquainted with a number of really outstanding motivational speakers—Dottie Walters, Denis Waitley, Cavett Roberts, Wayne Dyer, and of course, Zig Ziglar—and listened to their tapes (and read their books) regularly. By the time I got to the station, I was again excited about the possibilities of my new job. The goal would stay at $100,000.

To reach a goal, you have to believe it is possible. You decide on what it is, then get busy making it come true. We did have another meeting, but it was to reemphasize to everyone my belief that we could make it. Privately, I felt that even if we didn't reach the goal, we were better off setting it high.

As each day of September passed I could see the confidence and enthusiasm building among the staff. The techniques I had been teaching—the same ones I used myself—were working for them.

Then, at 4:30 P.M. on the final day of the month, the computer printed out the good news: Our billing total was $100,018. We'd made it with $18 to spare.

From that point on there was a feeling we could conquer the broadcast world. By December we were up to $140,000. Three months later the figure had climbed to $180,000. The following November we set a new record with $272,000 in billings. And all the while the station's listening audience grew very little.

We were fifteenth in the local ratings, but third in local ad billings.

Skipping up the Ladder

After I had increased sales almost 500 percent at the Dallas station I worked for, word began to spread quickly. In time Bruce Johnson, the president of Shamrock Broadcasting, wanted to test out my procedures. Fortunately, at the time I had no idea I was being tested (since tests were and still are something I've not fully conquered). He wanted to see if what I had done in Dallas was a fluke or if the technique could be used at other stations. He sent me to a station in Detroit and had me work with the sales force there. In relatively short order their sales went up—during a time when the economy of Detroit was at one of its all-time lows.

Then he sent me to Little Rock. Soon the station there was enjoying a 300 percent increase in sales. Everywhere I went sales improved, and frankly, it pleased me.

The interest shown me at corporate headquarters in Los Angeles caused me to start thinking of advancement possibilities. I liked the business and knew I wanted to climb higher on the corporate ladder. But there was a problem.

The logical sequence of advancement would go something like this: If you do well in sales, there is a chance to move up to a sales manager's position. If you're successful there, the opportunity to become a general manager might present itself. Doing a good job there might enable you to move up to a vice-presidency in charge of sales. All this, of course, takes time and a lot of hard work. But in my mind I saw myself as vice-president of sales for the Shamrock Broadcasting Company.

There was a stumbling block in the way of that ambition, however. Having reached the level of sales manager in a relatively short period, I knew my next logical step was to become a general manager. The role of general manager didn't interest me in the least. It is a desk job, concerned with bookkeeping, budgets, programming decisions—things like that. I simply could not see myself behind a desk all day, no longer dealing with people except when paperwork problems needed solving.

I was afraid I was stuck, and considered my situation unfair. Just because I knew nothing about programming and the purchase price of a new transmitter and didn't want to have to work up a station budget, why should I be blocked from my goal? I knew how to raise sales in any broadcast station.

Though unaware of it at the time, I solved my own problem by doing a good job as sales manager and in working with the other stations around the country. Bruce Johnson called me to his office. "Everywhere we've sent you," he said, "sales have gone up. We wanted to see if yours was an isolated situation there in Dallas or whether you had an approach that would work anywhere. You convinced us you know what you're doing. You are now vice-president in charge of sales for Shamrock Broadcasting.

Again, let me emphasize that things happen the day you decide you're going to make them happen. I knew my goal and I knew there was a roadblock in the way. But by doing my job to the best of my ability and maintaining confidence in myself and my capabilities I was able to jump past the general-manager difficulty and into the position I wanted. And one at which I felt I could do a good job.

I was a vice-president of Shamrock Broadcasting, owned by Disney—and had been in the business just two and a half years.

New Horizons

While I've repeatedly insisted that in order to make the advancement you hope for in life, the person you must depend on is you, it is a welcome bonus when the people around you share your enthusiasm.

Fortunately, the president of Shamrock was that kind of person. Bruce Johnson had a very positive attitude and provided me with additional confidence as I moved into my new job. He helped me believe in myself and immediately began forcing me to extend myself even further.

Though I'd never spoken to any group larger than a sales meeting, he had me take his place on the program at the annual meeting of the National Broadcasters Association, giving a speech to the third-largest convention in the United States.

He encouraged me to make an eighteen-city speaking tour, talking to radio broadcasters throughout the country. And all the while, the sales figures for the stations in the Shamrock system were climbing. I couldn't imagine things getting much better.

Then, in the spring of 1981, Bruce Johnson left Shamrock. The new president was far less aggressive, less enthusiastic. The entire organization took on a negative feel with which I was very uncomfortable.

In time I was offered a three-year contract, filled with restrictions I'd never dealt with before. It was time, I decided, to move on to something else. But what?

After I'd given it some thought, a new goal formed in my mind. I visualized it, worked out the pluses and minuses, and decided the time was right to begin working for myself. By that time I had given a grand total of two public speeches, but I decided I was going to form my own company and do sales and motivational speaking. Later on I began to do consulting work in the broadcasting field and was writing a monthly column for *Radio Only* magazine. I even did a series of broadcast sales tapes, outlining my own techniques.

Thus, Pam Lontos, Inc., was born on August 31, 1981 (Lontos Sales & Motivation, Inc., since 1986). Today I have an eight-member staff, a nice office, and a travel schedule that would drive anyone without wanderlust crazy. If someone had told me years earlier when I was shy and depressed that I would be speaking on platforms with Zig Ziglar, Paul Harvey, and Denis Waitley, I never would have believed it. At that point in my life when I was the most depressed, I thought no one would even want to talk to me. Now I've been on the *Phil Donahue* show, *PM Magazine, Hour Magazine,* because of the positive use of my subconscious mind.

A Whole New World

It has been a hectic, rewarding journey. It wasn't that long ago that I was a 160-pound, depressed housewife who slept eighteen hours a day and wore a size sixteen dress. I can still remember when I earned $750 a month teaching school and not enjoying myself at all.

There are times when I still think about those days when I was too shy even to speak when spoken to; when my self-image was so negative that suicide seemed the most logical solution to my problems. And I think back on my marriage (which finally ended in divorce in 1984 after several years of agonizing separation) and wonder why I allowed myself to get into and stay in such a position.

But I think back more in wonder than sorrow. Those were negative days and I no longer dwell on the negative. They were learning experiences—starting places really.

Since then, not only have I learned to help myself, I've learned to help others. That, perhaps, is the greatest reward of all. The opportunity to give, to share my opinions and feelings, has brought new meaning to my life, as well as the chance to meet a great number of wonderful people.

For instance, I was in Chicago not long ago to give a speech and afterward was approached by a charming lady who introduced herself as Agnes. We talked for some time and she told me how she and her husband had separated, she had lost a son, and was more depressed than she had ever been in her life. She wanted to find something constructive to do but was convinced she was too old. I recognized a lot of my old self in her and began telling her how I had been able to climb out of my own depression and make a place for myself in the working world.

"But what can a woman my age do?" she asked. "I have no experience but I really think I would like to try to sell real estate. The thing is, though, I've waited too long to do it. I'm afraid it's too late."

I encouraged her to forget about age and inexperience and begin seeing herself as that real estate agent—a successful one.

Today she is. And now she spreads the word. Her favorite saying, she tells me, is "Don't tell me it's impossible until after I've done it."

I hope, in time, it will become yours as well.

PART TWO

9

Everything in my whole life, then, has been a reflection of the picture I've had of myself. The bad and the good.

The reason I was so miserable for so long was that I had convinced myself I was worthless. But, as I would later learn, I wasn't worthless. Nor was I stupid and unable to accomplish anything. Those feelings were only the result of overwhelming negative thoughts I had carried with me for all too long.

Think as I did for long enough and your thoughts become the reality you are forced to live with. My reality, I assumed, was the life of a shy, overweight, depressed, unhappy person. And frankly, I did one heck of a job of playing the role.

Seeing no way to outrun the picture in my subconscious mind, I resigned myself to my fate. Such is the frightening power of the subconscious in determining how you choose to feel and how you deal with other people and situations.

Let me illustrate my point with an exercise I've found effective (if possible, have someone read the following instructions to you):

Imagine you have in front of you a nice, cold, juicy lemon. Next to it is a knife. Now, pick up the lemon and hold it in your hand in front of you. The lemon is very cold. Your hand, in turn, is getting cold. You're also feeling the weight of the lemon as you hold it. Gradually, it is getting heavier.

With a finger of your other hand, feel the outside of the lemon. Feel the cold, rough texture of it.

Now set the lemon back onto the table and pick up the imaginary knife. Cut the lemon in half. It's so juicy that it is dripping all over the table. Imagine that you can see the juice of that lemon.

Pick up one half of the lemon and squeeze it. Let the juice run down your hand and arm. Now smell the lemon. Lick it and taste it.

Unless you're far different from most people, you now have a mouthful of saliva. Why? Because, during the exercise, your brain sent a message to your mouth to produce saliva to wash away the acid of the lemon juice. A lemon that wasn't even really there.

If the subconscious mind is so powerful that it can send a message like that, doesn't it make sense to try to use it in a constructive, positive manner?

How to Achieve Threefold Reward with Half the Work

There is always a physical manifestation of what you have in your subconscious mind. It is, then, reasonable to assume that whatever you program the mind to think is what will happen. Adopt a "can't do" attitude and it is a good bet that you can't. The opposite also applies.

On occasion we can play tricks on our subconscious. We can, if we try hard enough, outrun those negative images. But only for a while. That's why you see some people go on a diet, take off pounds, then, once the goal is accomplished, immediately begin to put the weight back on. Subconsciously, they have never believed they could and should be thinner. Or a salesman who, with a burst of energy and hard work, has the best month of his career, far exceeding his own personal best. Once done, though, he doubts his ability to maintain that kind of pace. The next month he drops back to mediocre production.

These people return to the negative picture in the subconscious mind. And the pattern will continue until that picture, that image, is changed to a more positive one.

Trying to achieve a goal without first getting the proper picture of success in your mind will result in a great deal of stress and frustration. I know; I tried it.

When I first went to work I was the perfect example of the workaholic. Wanting so badly to succeed, to reestablish my self-worth, I put in long hours and worried constantly. Though I enjoyed what I was doing, I never felt I could relax. If I had a client on this side of town, I needed to see him right away so that I could rush to the other side of town and keep another appointment. There were times when I felt I was running everywhere and getting nowhere. I was making money, getting my job done, but it was making a nervous wreck of me.

My problem was that I was still battling with my subconscious. The tired, defeated, self-conscious image I had long had of myself was still at work. There was a small, whispered voice telling me that I really wasn't supposed to make a go of what I was doing. That inner struggle was what was producing the stress, making me nervous. So fearful was I of failure that I overdid. I used up more energy than was necessary but didn't get as much accomplished as I should have, trying to compensate for feelings about myself that I had not yet been able to cast out.

When I finally did, there was a dramatic change. With the picture altered from negative to positive, my sales tripled even as I expended only half the energy I previously had. Relaxed, more confident, I found I could get things done in a more methodical, professional way. The helter-skelter lack of system, the nerve-racking rush weren't necessary—as my subconscious had been telling me for so long.

I'd like for you to do another exercise. Again, it will help to have someone read the instructions to you.

Close your eyes. Put both hands out in front of you, palms up. Keeping your eyes closed, try to tune out everything except the voice reading you these instructions. Try to imagine vividly the scene you're being told about.

Hold your arms straight out in front of you, shoulder high. Don't bend your elbows. Imagine that in your right hand I'm placing a large volume of the *Encyclopaedia Britannica*. You're holding that heavy book in your right hand. To your left hand we've tied a string and connected it to the ceiling so that you have to expend no effort at all to keep it straight out in front of you.

Now, in your right hand I'm placing two more volumes of the encyclopedia. You now have the weight of those three books to deal with. In the meantime, we've pulled up on the string attached to your left hand, providing it even more support—to a point where you can, in fact, totally relax your left hand.

Now we're adding a fourth book to the load you're already holding in your right hand. The string attached to your left hand is pulled even higher, making your entire arm rise toward the ceiling.

Finally, we place two more books in your right hand. Imagine yourself holding them for a minute while I slowly count backward from ten to one. When the counting is completed, you may open your eyes.

What you will find is that your hands are no longer at equal height. Your left hand, the one supported by the imaginary string, is higher than the right hand, which has been supporting all that make-believe weight. Probably the muscles in your right shoulder and arm even feel tight.

Once again, your subconscious has been hard at work, showing you its awesome power. Doesn't it make sense to have that power working *for* you, rather than against you?

Desire Is the First Major Step

It is the desire to achieve, to accomplish goals, that creates that electrical current and power within us. Volumes have been written on the advantages of positive thinking. I choose to think of it as "positive believing." By believing something can happen—whether for good or ill—we can greatly enhance the probability that it *will* happen.

I've noticed that if I'm lukewarm about something, if I don't really have a strong desire to finish a particular task, chances are that I won't. On the other hand, if I make up my mind to succeed at something, to make it happen, my chances are greatly enhanced. Remember, belief must be followed by *action!*

Desire, of course, can't accomplish the impossible. And, as I said early on in this book, there are no promises of miracles. You must have the capability within yourself to reach your chosen aim. Ability, matched with desire and hard work, is necessary. I could not, for instance, wish myself into the role of gifted doctor or astronaut for the simple reason that I lack the abilities required in those professions.

By the same token, each of us has talent we've seldom if ever even considered using. The first step toward bringing that talent into the open is the desire to do so. The desire unleashes the frustrations brought on by unused ability, and sets the ability into motion.

Desire, used realistically, is the first weapon we have available to us. Absolutely nothing of a positive nature can be accomplished without our first having the desire to accomplish. Some of us, unfortunately, have our desires locked so deep within us that we have difficulty realizing we even have them. They may be hard to find at times. But they're there. And each individual must seek out his or her own.

Then, having found the desire, you must match it with your capabilities. Once that marriage of desire and ability is made, a big step in the right direction has been taken. You have added power to your emotions.

And it is important to remember this: The very fact that you express a desire is proof that you do have the capability.

Remove the Block

It is essential to recognize that latent ability is what causes us to want to do more, to make something of ourselves that at present we are not. The simple fact that you are making no move in that direction is indication that a block exists. It must be removed—by looking deeply into yourself to determine exactly what you wish to make of your life. Tune out the voices that tell you, you can't do it. Focus on the goal; summon the desire to achieve it; then devise a route that will get you there.

It was famed psychologist William James who said, "The greatest discovery of my generation is that human beings can alter their lives by altering their attitude of mind."

With that one twenty-word sentence, he has summed up the essence of this entire book.

Dreaming the "Impossible" Dream

One of the quickest and most certain avenues you can travel to achieve opportunity in life is to elevate your dreams above your reality. If your dreams and your reality are the same, there is no conflict, nor is there any forward movement. There is no drive, no reason to try to move ahead.

Whether we recognize it or not, each of us has a "comfort zone." Within certain boundaries we've subconsciously set for ourselves, we can be reasonably content and even happy. We make up our minds that we deserve just so much happiness, so much security, so much money. If unwilling to venture beyond those boundaries, we will never move ahead.

Sadly, there are millions who have locked themselves into a comfort zone, with no desire ever to get out. If they do, by some stroke of luck, attain more than they feel they deserve, whether it be financial gain or happiness, they immediately become worried about losing it—and, almost without exception, they step back into the way of life their minds are better able to deal with. That's why it's called a "comfort zone."

There are those who would rather be comfortable with less achievement than take the risk of reaching for a higher level which while improving their lives, might make more demands on them.

I challenge you to show me a high achiever who is so security-oriented, so concerned that everything be stable and risk-free, that he or she won't take a chance by putting dreams on a level above reality.

Only after you've committed yourself to that chance-taking philosophy will you find the drive necessary for success.

The following exercise demonstrates what I mean:

> Put your right hand straight out in front of you and say, "Here's reality." Then raise your left hand a foot or two higher and say, "Here are my dreams."

Once you realize that your dreams and reality are not on the same level, you will find yourself faced with a conflict. Conflict, then, breeds frustration. And that frustration, finally, will spur you to action, to begin contemplating ways by which you can do more.

Resolving the conflict isn't going to be easy. There will be obstacles along the way. In many cases, once the first obstacle is faced, people give up and lower their dreams back to their reality. This is one way to resolve the conflict. Only those with the strength to persist will break through.

There is such a thing as positive stress—or positive frustration. Without it, we would not have the stimulation or excitement to create and grow. The truth of the matter is, a life totally without frustration or stress would be pretty boring.

It is generally when we find ourselves in a rut or confronted by some obstacle that we encounter stress. But stress is one of those negatives that can be turned into a positive, a motivation tool. To put it behind us, we work harder. The stress, it turns out, has become the "starter" we needed.

And we're on our way toward bringing our reality up out of the comfort zone, to match our dreams.

10

I know little about the magic of science, but it is my firm belief that our self-image is greatly affected by the power of that magic. Let me explain:

If you took an iron bar, placed it in the middle of an empty room, and started it vibrating, after a while it would give off a humming sound. The more the vibration, the greater the sound and the higher the pitch. If the vibration continued to increase, the bar would eventually give off warmth. As it got hotter and hotter, it would begin to change color. The metallic color would turn to red, then eventually to white heat. Theoretically, it would pass on into an ultraviolet-light stage and ultimately into invisible X rays.

In time, scientists tell us, the vibration would produce electromagnetic waves which are neither visible nor audible without benefit of sophisticated equipment. What is interesting is that those electromagnetic waves were there, in a dormant stage, from the moment the bar was placed in the room. For them to be activated, however, the high-speed vibration and heating process was necessary.

The workings of our minds are much the same. Our thought patterns are—and this is a simplified explanation—electromagnetic waves of an even higher scale. The entire body, in fact, is a magnificent electronic force field. Thought patterns are passed by electrical impulses that move from one neuron cell in the brain to another. When you think to wiggle your little toe, for instance, the thought travels from the brain by electrical impulses, down through a series of nerves until it reaches that toe.

The Magic Is in the Mind

There is a power in the mind that we never really use unless we learn to. Only after we realize the energy and possibilities our mind affords us can we progress toward its better use.

I've come in contact with literally hundreds of people who are unwilling to accept the fact that you can, to a certain degree, program your own mind. The very idea seems too far-out, too akin to science fiction. Yet it is possible—and not really that difficult once you've decided to do it.

For example: Let's say you've spent your entire life being painfully shy and want to become a more outgoing sort of person. The first step is to make up your mind that you want to change. Every day you visualize yourself as a more outgoing, smiling person, one whom people are readily drawn to. You see yourself as a more confident person. By visualizing a new you again and again, thinking positively about the personality change you hope to effect, you leave an imprint in your mind. In time that imprint becomes so firmly established that it is more reality than fantasy. In your mind's eye, you do, in fact, become a more outgoing, pleasant, confident person. The shyness begins to disappear. You have to reprogram your mind from negative to positive.

It is as if you have actually experienced that which you wish to be. And, as we've all been taught, experience is the best teacher.

With enough mental preparation, the change becomes not only a possibility but a reality. And the ball really begins to roll. Once you see the first signs of success—a smiling hello to someone you've never spoken to before, for instance—you gain confidence in the process. You begin to tell yourself: "This really does work."

And, eventually, you'll get a reaction from others that is even more convincing. When you reach out to others, you'll find them reaching out to you. The sender and the receiver have become active. And the change you've made in yourself will activate a change in others.

Some call that science. I think it's magical and wonderful!

You Make Your Own Luck

When I had no real friends and a rock-bottom self-image, I blamed everyone but myself for my plight. It never occurred to me that I was the one tuning others out of my life.

What I didn't realize was that what we think about ourselves prompts a response from other people. Unfortunately, most people are prone to agree with others. So, if we think we're neither personable nor interesting, it's easy to find a lot of people eager to accept that estimate as fact.

Why is it that certain people have charisma and others don't? How is it that there can be some people at a party who are obviously popular and seem to draw others to them naturally, comfortably, while there are other people whom no one seems to want to be around? Why is it that it seems easy to spot a depressed person and avoid his or her company? Why, by the same token, are we drawn to those who seem happy and energetic?

Again, the signals being sent out affect our relationships. A cheerful person wants to stay that way and therefore makes an effort to avoid anyone who is depressed. No one actively seeks out an avenue to depression. Given a choice, he or she will gravitate to the company of someone who appears to be happy; someone who can share that happiness.

What I'm saying is: We do pick up the thoughts of others. The signals are sent out and we have the option of various reactions. The signals you send out, then, will directly affect the way you are treated by others.

If you've conditioned your mind properly, you're one of the lucky ones. You've made up your mind to view yourself and the world around you in a positive light and others are drawn to you, adding their own positive views, reinforcing what you think of yourself.

You don't just stumble into luck like that, however. You must create it yourself, working at it constantly.

So First You Change the Picture

One of the greatest mistakes people make is rushing into action before they really have any idea about what direction they're headed in. They decide one day to make some changes in their personality and get busy right away. The problem is, they haven't any really firm idea of what they want to become. They only know they don't like what they are.

The second order of business, after the decision to change has been made, is to alter the picture you carry of yourself in your own mind. Already you're aware of the present picture: You're shy; you're overweight; you lack self-confidence. Begin formulating a picture of what you want to be: outgoing, trim, confident. Run that new image over and over in your mind. Make sure the goal is something you can visualize, something whose reality you can come to believe in with all your heart. Then go into action.

By taking it step by step you can avoid the pitfall William James warns us of: "Whenever there's a conflict between will and the subconscious, the subconscious always wins." To be a winner, you first have to make sure your will is strong enough to defeat that subconscious image that's been lodged in the back of your brain for so long. It is no easy task; and it won't happen overnight. In a sense, you've got to give yourself constant pep talks, convincing yourself that you know for certain who you want to be and that you've got a good plan for getting there.

First, though, that picture has to be vivid. In a way, you're looking into your own future, seeing the person you want to become.

Then the actual changes can begin.

Becoming the Person in Your Mind

You now can picture yourself as what you want to be. You see yourself as thin, eating the proper foods, getting the right amount of exercise. To attain those goals takes effort. No one in history ever thought herself thin. She had to call up the will to change her diet, to forget about chocolate cake, to get up off the sofa and begin jogging or doing aerobics. The same applies to those whose goal is to be less shy, or earn more money, or enjoy a better sex life.

Day in and day out you have to work on your mind. You convince yourself that you will, no matter what, become the person you picture yourself being. Then you go to work at getting there.

In time, then, the picture and the action begin to match. They work hand-in-hand, each providing momentum for the other. The clearer the picture, the harder you work; the harder you work, the clearer the picture becomes.

Too, the stress engendered by your recognition of the gap between your dreams and your reality disappears. If you take the time first to change that negative picture of yourself, to forget about the old you and focus your attention on the aspired-to new you, it is much easier. Why? Because the picture and the action are not in conflict. Confident in the knowledge of where you're going and aware that you're making headway getting there, you won't have to battle with the stress and frustration that accompany uncertain moves and motivations.

A person with a plan, then, is more organized. The steps you've got to take are neatly set out in 1-2-3 order and you're able to chart the distance you've come. Perhaps most important, you'll be able to realize it when you've finally attained the goal you've set for yourself.

There are no shortcuts. Before taking action, it is imperative that you know what you're trying to do. And, reaching that awareness—seeing that picture clearly—can take every bit as much time as the actual carrying out of your actions.

11

During my battle with depression, I thought often about suicide. In all honesty, I think the only thing that prevented me from following through was that I simply lacked the requisite energy.

There was a time when all I wanted to do was lie in bed reading. Then even reading became a chore and I would just lie there staring at the ceiling. More times than I like to think about, I considered getting up, walking to the medicine cabinet, and taking enough sleeping pills to put me out of my misery. But, thank God, I wasn't able to muster the strength to make that short trip.

Finally, as I've mentioned, I hit bottom. I came to a point in my life where the alternatives seemed crystal clear: either kill myself, or get out of bed and try to change my life. That was the day I made the most important decision I've ever made. I decided I wanted to live—but not in the miserable condition I had allowed myself to become locked into.

Later, as I read, studied, and researched, I came to the realization that even a change for the better can be a stressful process. Change, in and of itself, creates stress.

Only when we accept the fact that stress is going to be a day-to-day part of our lives, and that to move forward we must be able to deal with it, can we really begin to make progress.

When you finally make that decision to make a positive change in your life, you must *face the truth about yourself:* Accept the fact that you're never going to be free of stress. Any change in your life is going to produce it. Say you've been offered a better job with an income double what you're now making. It has to be an exciting proposition. On the other hand, let's assume you're reasonably comfortable with your current job. You have the opportunity for a positive step up, yet you're not sure you want to take it. The decision, whether to take the job or to stay in the one you now have, will be accompanied by stress.

What you need to realize is that the stress is not a negative sign. It is a natural human response, one that has to be dealt with.

Why do we so often resist change, even when it is obviously for our own betterment? Quite often it is because we don't want to admit we've been doing the wrong thing for years. Perhaps you have stayed with a secure job, never really enjoying it or finding it rewarding. Maybe you've clung to a personal relationship even though deep down you know it is bad for you. But to make the change, even though it holds promise of a better life, would require an admission that a lot of years have been wasted.

Too often it is more comfortable to live with false thinking than to admit you've just been kidding yourself; that you have, in fact, been wasting your time and energies pursuing the wrong way of life for you.

None of us enjoys being forced to admit we've wasted

our time. But if it is true, the sooner the admission is made and accepted, the sooner we can get on with the business of making sure no more time is wasted.

Reaching the point where you can face the truth about your situation is no easy task. Once you've admitted things aren't the way you want them to be, however, you begin to realize that you are the one who has the right to choose your own happiness.

Truth Hurts

When I was struggling to deal with my own depression, beginning work at the health club, the owner gave me a set of tapes by Zig Ziglar titled "How to Stay Motivated."

At first I listened to them out of curiosity, not really knowing what to believe. In time, though, there was one statement made by Ziglar that really made an impression on me, that opened a door and made it possible for me to understand everything else he was saying.

It was in the middle of the afternoon and I was stretched out on the sofa, afraid that I was not going to make it as a salesperson and was going to slide back into the blackness of the depression I'd begun to battle. Ziglar said, "People say that you pay the price for success, but really you don't. You pay the price for failure!"

At that very moment I realized that was what I was doing. I was paying the price for my failures. I was over thirty years old and getting nowhere. Worse, I had no one willing to help me, to rescue me from myself and my situation.

The price for my failures, I determined, was far too high. It dawned on me as I listened to Zig Ziglar's voice that I was the only one who could change the way I was living.

Only then was I really able to face the truth about myself. The time had come to stop blaming others for my unhappiness. The first step was to become more independent. Soon I found myself moving—slowly but surely—in a new and exciting direction.

The Cause and Solution: Internal, Not External

Just what is it that is stopping you from attaining the things that you want?

The answer, most likely, is you. The problems are internal, not external. It is easy to blame a boss or a family member or a so-called friend for your misfortunes and unhappiness, but such blame-placing solves no problems. It doesn't even address the real problem.

Quit blaming others and accept the responsibility yourself. The problem lies within, so a close self-examination is necessary. Look at your problems and see how they relate to you, not to others. Determine the changes you need to make.

This isn't going to be easy. None of us wants to admit we're wrong. We don't want to hear we're in the wrong line of work or living with the wrong person or choosing the wrong friends. We don't want to admit we're living our lives the wrong way. An overwhelming negative statement about our own life—a life we're supposed to be able to control—is difficult to come to grips with.

But until we accept the fault as our own, we're stymied. Blaming others gets us nowhere.

Sink or Swim

It is essential that you adopt a critical stance about yourself. Look at yourself in the mirror and determine what you really see, not what you want to see. Take a long, hard look at your environment, your surroundings, your associates, your attitudes. Then ask yourself: "Is this everything I want? Is this my idea of perfection? Is this the answer to my dreams?"

If not, accept the shortcomings you see. Admit they're your own fault, and begin making plans for change. That's how you take charge of your life: not by fooling yourself about the identity of that person in the mirror, not by blaming others for the problems you've found impossible to cope with.

Only when you've come to grips with those truths can the change begin. That's the moment you actually begin to take charge.

By admitting that you are the root of your own problems, you open the door to your own well-being, your own happiness. You will realize, finally, that you have the cure within yourself.

I make no promise that it will work magically the very first time you gather strength to take a hard look at your own role in your unhappiness. Admitting fault and assuming responsibility is difficult, even for self-assured people. You must work at it. And then, when you think you're making some slight progress, work even harder.

The effort will be worth it.

12

A timeworn but worthy piece of advice suggests we can do nothing about the past and have only minimal control over the future, so we'd best devote our efforts to making the most we can of the present. Largely, I agree—particularly with the part about the past.

Apart from using bygone experience as a learning tool, there is nothing this side of the invention of a time machine that will enable us to alter those things—good or bad—we've already been through.

On the other hand, I strongly believe we can have a dramatic effect on our future if we work hard at making the best of the present. It is now, today, that we establish goals for the future. Today we dream the dreams we hope will come true tomorrow.

We must, however, walk a fine line. Too much attention to the future and we lose track of the demands of the present. That can become as big a problem as dwelling on the past.

I've known too many people who have spent most of their lives worried either about things that have already happened or about what might yet happen—or both—never paying attention to what is happening in their lives at present. They are, in a sense, in limbo, always looking backward or forward, but really going nowhere.

The present moment is when we should deal with our problems—which is not to say that they will all be magically solved before five o'clock closing. But by making up our minds to deal with them, now, we've set something positive in motion.

If we take affirmative action today, we can reasonably expect some future benefit.

The Past Is Gone—Drop It

There is absolutely no logical reason for dwelling on (or in) the past. It will neither solve your problems today nor answer your questions about tomorrow. Reflecting on negative experiences makes them that much harder to escape. They clutter your mind and sap the energy and willpower you need to handle the uncertainties of today.

Of course I'm not suggesting you try to block out the past totally. That would be not only foolish but impossible. There are too many memories that have become personal touchstones for us: first dates, the birth of children, awards, successes, and myriad bittersweet moments dear to us all.

What I'm talking about are those negative things which, when recalled, tend to lead to depression. Worrying forever about getting fired from a past job won't help you keep the one you have now and is unlikely to help you get a better one in future.

Reflecting on such bad experiences reinflames the subconscious fears we have of our own shortcomings, forcing us to focus on them rather than the positives. The truth of the matter is that fear tends to distort. A bygone problem that was, in truth, relatively minor can grow to monstrous size if we allow it to.

At the risk of getting a bit romantic, think of this: Most women, I think, remember that first good-night kiss, remember it as a sweet, tender moment when a marvelous new world opened to them. What we do—and, yes, I'm as guilty as the next person—is romanticize. In truth, the whole situation was probably incredibly awkward, didn't feel that great, and embarrassed both parties. That wasn't Robert Redford kissing me passionately on the front porch when I was fifteen years old. It was Harvey Betwiler, and his glasses poked me in the nose when our lips finally did meet. No big deal, really.

See what I mean? Distortion, even of something very positive. The same works for negative reflections—in spades.

For those who have developed a fear of the past, allowing it to control their actions in the present, I would suggest they consider this: F-E-A-R stands for False Evidence Appearing Real.

Commit to Today

Another factor toward changing your life, then, is a strong determination to make the best of your life today. You've decided who you want to be and there is no time like the present to become that person. Forget about those long years of shyness: Smile instead. Forget about being forty pounds overweight: Start to diet today. Forget about the office manager who said there were no openings last week: Go knock on some more doors today.

The moment you decide to change is the most important. Concentrate your attention and your energies on the small time frame of today—and tomorrow will take care of itself.

The decision, really, is the hard part. That's what you've got to accomplish first—today. Once that commitment is made, the rest comes much easier. In retrospect, you'll be able to admit that the day you actually decided to trim down or quit smoking or become more independent was even more important than the day the goal was finally reached. That's the day it *really* happened!

Today is the most important day you'll ever live. And if you approach it that way, your tomorrows can be what you've always hoped for.

13

It is impossible to get what you really want out of life unless you know specifically what you're after. Without tangible goals, you have no real target to shoot for. Too often, people who decide they want to change their lives will work toward putting themselves in a positive frame of mind, but have no real plan of attack. An "I can do" attitude is good, but unless you can see in your mind what you're after, positive thinking won't get the job done.

What is needed is a good supply of "positive believing." Once your goals are set, you can convince yourself that you're going to reach them.

Goal setting, then, should be a very specific thing. The percentage of people who want to accomplish things—losing weight, becoming a better person, climbing the corporate ladder—is very high, but studies show that less than 4 percent actually set specific goals they wish to reach.

The problem is that most people just don't realize the goal is necessary if one is to maintain the momentum and enthusiasm necessary to get there. Be specific. If you want to lose weight, determine exactly how much you want to weigh. If you want to earn a better income, assign a dollar figure to that ambition.

If You Can't See It, You Won't Get It

The most productive form of imagination is vivid, filled with specific detail. It is imperative that you visualize, have a definite picture in your mind. Simply stating that you want to earn more money isn't enough. Decide how much more. Then your statement will be something like this: "I want to increase my income to $100,000 this year." You have in your mind's eye a figure to work toward.

Let me give you an example:

When I speak to groups, I often suggest they think of a car they would like to have. Each of us will envision a different kind of car, of course. But most of the group will generally say something about a "new car." Some may even go so far as to name a particular make and model. But few ever really get down to specifics. What color do they want it to be? How much horsepower? What about gas mileage? Two-door or four-door?

If you're really serious about getting a new car—if that's one of your goals—you've got to deal in specifics. You must have a strong, detailed mental image of what it is you want.

The importance of that mental image is based on the function of something called the reticular activating system, or RAS, which is located at the base of the brain. It is a filtering system which allows those things important to your existence to come into your mind while at the same time, it filters out things that are unimportant. It is the reason we're able to concentrate on certain things and ignore others. Without the RAS, for instance, you would hear all the noise and conversations going on at a party rather than being able to focus your attention on whomever you're talking with directly.

On the other hand, even if you're engaged in a conversation, you will hear your name called from the other side of the room. Your brain is programmed to let that call through the filtering system—because it is something specific, something important.

Which is to say, we're programmed, whether we realize it or not, to specifics. So why not take full advantage of that fact?

Another example: A mother might be sleeping near her sick baby. Outside, a fire engine screams past. In the living room the other children are watching television with the volume tuned too high. But the mother, tired from being up most of the night with her sick child, sleeps on, unaware.

Then the baby wakes and begins softly to cry. Immediately, the mother wakes. Why? Because her mind was programmed to the importance of the safety and comfort of her child. The reticular activating system allowed that cry through while filtering out the unimportant noises.

How many times have you seen a new word while reading or heard the name of a city unfamiliar to you, then found in the next week or so that the word or name came to your attention on several occasions? Once you've allowed it to gain entry into your mind, it is established there. You'll be aware of it. It is no longer filtered out because, for whatever reason, you chose to attach some importance to it. It was all there before, you just didn't notice it. It's the same thing with what we call luck: Opportunities are all around you to obtain all you want to have and accomplish in life. However, unless you program your reticular activating system for them, you won't see them.

The human brain, still one of the world's greatest scientific mysteries, is capable of incredible things. Using it to help establish specific goals, in fact, would have to be judged one of the simpler tasks we ask of it.

Long-term and Short-term Goals

To plan the new future you're looking ahead to, both long-term and short-term goals are necessary.

The long-term goals, those which may take a considerable amount of time to reach, are, in effect, your dreams. They may be a year or longer in the making.

But because they take more time and, generally, more hard work to reach, the long-term goals have to be supplemented by short-term goals. Short-term achievements, those things that take a few days or weeks to accomplish, are not only stepping-stones but great morale boosters. Positive accomplishment, however slight, gives us the momentum to continue striving toward our longer-range goals.

In the Summary section at the end of this book you'll find a Goal Planning Guide. On it, I want you to write down two long-term goals and two short-term goals. Above each of them write the reward you plan to give yourself for its achievement. Then, regardless of what that reward might be—a new dress, a stereo for the car—be sure you follow through. Don't try to play tricks on your own mind and renege on the promised reward once the goal is attained. If you do, your subconscious will get into the act quickly and will quit helping.

When I was still sales manager at the radio station and had set a goal of $100,000 in sales that particular month, I told myself that if we reached that figure, I'd buy myself a large-screen television set. When we made our goal, I began to think to myself: *I've got a little problem here. That reward I promised myself costs plenty. Should I go through with it?*

The answer was clearly yes, for several reasons. First, I

had used that TV set as a kind of imaginary carrot, dangling just out of reach all month. Then, there was the difficulty that not giving myself that reward was sure to cause.

If I hadn't kept my promise to myself, my chances of succeeding in a goal/reward situation the next time would have been nil. My subconscious mind would have told me: "I'm not helping you this time. Last month you promised me a present, and I helped you toward your goal. I got you through those tired days. I helped you find the right thing to say to a customer. I did everything I could to give you support because you had promised me a reward. But you didn't keep your word. Don't expect my help next month."

So whatever the reward you set for yourself, get it. No excuses. If the car breaks down and needs repair, don't let that stand in the way of your reward. Believe me, it will be far more important to you than a new transmission in the long run.

Another helpful idea: As you're thinking about what your goals should be, play some music that you enjoy. A nice song with lyrics you particularly like or a beat that makes you feel good stimulates your brain to produce endorphins, naturally occurring substances that can help you get in an "up" frame of mind.

Be Specific

So let's start using the powers we have. Decide what it is you want and be specific. Decide you want to lose eighteen pounds. Decide you want an apple-red Porsche convertible with white seat covers and a stereo tape deck. Make up your mind that you want a certain house in a certain neighborhood in a certain price range.

Let's say a new house is your goal. If you haven't already seen that particular dream house with a FOR SALE sign out front, you need to determine what the house of your dreams looks like. It's important that you have a picture of it in your mind. Look through magazines for it. Drive around, and if you find a likely prospect, snap a photograph of it to keep with you. Before any dream or ambition can become a reality, it must be vividly pictured in your mind's eye. Once visualized and fixed there, it becomes the magnet that pulls it in.

The good old reticular activating system—sounds like something out of a *Star Trek* rerun, doesn't it?—takes over. Once your mind is programmed, what you want is no longer filtered out but comes through loud and clear—because it has become important to you. On the other hand, if you don't have a clear picture in your mind, the RAS isn't going to help you. Only when you are specific about every little detail does the real importance of the goal register as it should.

Taking Bite-Size Pieces

If your goal is to lose sixteen pounds, you begin by saying you want to lose exactly that. You know full well that isn't going to happen overnight, so you reduce the goal into bite-size, attainable portions. Break it down like this: You're going to lose sixteen pounds in eight weeks. That means you're going to lose two pounds a week. Suddenly you have a goal that is not only realistic but one whose progress you can track. No longer is the idea of losing sixteen pounds overwhelming. All you're talking about is two pounds a week.

Next, you begin to picture yourself as slim. Visualize how you'll look in a certain dress or swimsuit. With that image in mind, you'll be far less likely to make those late-night trips to the refrigerator. That bowl of ice cream is no longer as important as the image of a thin you.

Back when I was overweight and first trying to do

something about the size sixteen I had grown to, I found a great-looking photograph of Farrah Fawcett in a magazine. She was wearing a bikini and looked stunning. Carefully I clipped out just my head from a snapshot of me and pasted it over Farrah Fawcett's head. I put the composite photo on the refrigerator door. Every day I saw myself as thin, trim, and pretty darn sexy-looking.

I admit that I never became any real threat to Farrah, but the little picture trick helped; it provided an additional bit of motivation.

I've heard of people trying to accomplish the same thing by placing photographs of a really fat person on the refrigerator as a motivational aid. The thinking, I suppose, is to be able to say to yourself: "I don't want to look like that!" In most cases, though, the person probably already looks more like that than they do like Farrah Fawcett. To me, that's a negative approach.

Don't waste time visualizing what you don't want to be. Picture what you want to become.

Reprogramming the RAS

When you go window-shopping, picture yourself in the size eight your sixteen-pound weight loss is going to get you back into. Constantly remind yourself that soon you're going to be a size eight. Make it the dominant thought in your mind. If you stop to look at dresses, look at the size-eight rack, nowhere else.

It is at this point that your reticular activating system begins to offer help. You've convinced yourself you're going to get down to that particular size, and the RAS is ready to allow that idea into your thought patterns.

Conversely, if you haven't vividly pictured yourself as thinner—the way you're going to be after those sixteen pounds are gone—something entirely different is going to happen on your shopping trips. As you walk from store to store, you're going to be drawn to those shops selling a wonderful variety of cheeses or even giving away free food samples. You'll see the ice-cream shop, the chocolate cookies on sale—and the idea of food will become dominant. That's what your RAS will attract.

Only after you've fully dedicated yourself to weight loss and begun to see yourself as the thin person you'll become will such thoughts be blocked out.

The same thing happens when you pick up a magazine or watch television. If you haven't been specific about your diet plans, you're going to notice the food ads and commercials. And the first thing you know, you're headed for the kitchen.

Such is the importance of a mental picture. It can work for you in a negative or positive manner. The choice is yours. The makers of a particular brand of pizza know how to make food important to you while you're watching TV late at night. They offer you a beautiful picture, right?

You've got to do the same thing with your plan for losing weight. And it has to be as specific as the ingredients shown you in the pizza commercial. Just to say you're going to lose weight doesn't bring any picture to mind. But to say you're going to lose sixteen pounds and get into a size eight does.

Once you've reached that point, the food shops, the magazine ads, and the TV commercials are less important. Your will to lose weight negates the hunger you previously felt because the dominant thing in your mind is getting rid of those pounds.

But it happens only when you've become specific about your goal.

Focusing on the Positive

It is often very difficult for people to decide what they specifically want. On the other hand, it seems relatively easy to decide what they don't want. It is a matter of priorities out of sequence.

You've heard someone—perhaps yourself—say, "I'm sick of my old car. It doesn't run well, looks awful, has developed all kinds of mechanical troubles, and is costing me a fortune in repair bills and gas." That's the negative approach, true though it may be.

Only when they say, "My car's a wreck; I'm going to get rid of it and get me a new one," are they switching to the positive and becoming specific.

For a long time I drove a car that looked like a demolition-derby reject. I had bought it secondhand for just a couple of hundred dollars, so you can imagine the shape it was in. But at the time, I was comfortable with it because my self-image was so low that the car seemed a perfect match. Getting a nicer car never even entered my mind. It was outside my comfort zone.

But after I got into radio sales and found that I had to drive all over town to visit clients, my car's lack of air conditioning began to concern me. In the summer months I would arrive at an appointment looking wilted and wind-blown.

After two years of driving that clunker (the radio didn't even play), it occurred to me that I needed a better car. In fact, I began to realize that I *deserved* a better car, one with air conditioning, a good radio, and some comfort. I began to visualize myself in a new car. In time it became a silver Corvette.

Then I ran into another roadblock. After deciding what kind of car I wanted, I began looking into what it would cost. To be able to afford it, I realized, I would have to increase my sales.

What I did was apply the same step-by-step principle that works for weight loss. The cost of the car was $14,000. The monthly payments would be $350. To afford that monthly expense, I would have to make only one additional sale per month.

By breaking down the expense of a new car into monthly payments, then determining what I would have to do month-to-month to afford it, I made the whole idea realistic.

As a plus, it gave me an additional incentive to improve my sales each month.

Extra Effort Can Be Easy

In effect, I was putting things into a more manageable perspective. I reduced the situation from (a) the total price of the car to (b) the monthly payments to (c) what I would have to do to be certain I could afford the payments.

My next step was to make a dream chart and place it on my wall. On it was a picture of the car I wanted. Seeing it every day made me want it all the more; thus I was motivated to increase my sales.

On a normal working day, I would generally head back for the station at around 4:00 P.M. I decided I would work an extra hour every day until I was convinced that the additional income I needed was possible. I made up my mind to stay a little longer with some of those borderline clients who were close to buying but needed a little additional persuasion. And it worked.

In a sense, then, getting a new car—my dream car—cost me one extra day's work a week.

Once I had the car, I found that it was a great motivator. If the weather was bad and I really didn't want to be running all over town on slick roads or in pouring rain, I went anyway—because in the back of my mind I knew I had to make that car payment at the end of the month. It became a wonderful incentive.

By working just a little harder I not only raised my income to a point where I could afford the car, but considerably higher. A chain reaction had set in.

The desire to buy the car had forced me to work harder.

And by working harder I was earning considerably more money. Thus, what I really did was raise what I like to call my "comfort level." Instead of making five calls a day on clients, I was making as many as ten. Instead of leaving the station at 11:00 A.M. to begin making sales calls, I was out the door by 9:30 because I was eager to get into my new car.

When I arrived at an appointment I was in good spirits. And because of that I came across as far more confident than I had back when I was driving the clunker that I was never certain would get me there.

The new enthusiasm had greater effect than I could have imagined. Concerned about upping my monthly income by $350, I found that I had increased it by $2,250. Shoot, the Corvette was free. If I hadn't bought it in the first place, my sales would never have taken the jump they did. Because I had made the decision to buy it, I was clearing almost an additional $2,000—after making the monthly payment to the auto dealer.

Suddenly I had more money to put into savings or investments or to buy new clothes.

That's when I became convinced that the specific-reward principle was one of the most important tools available to anyone trying to change his or her life.

Once you determine on a specific goal and dedicate yourself to achieving it, your energies and emotions quickly pitch in. Then it becomes much easier than you ever would have thought.

14

If you are working daily to reprogram your mind, avoiding the negatives and believing that you can in fact improve your life, if you've faced the truth about yourself and decided what you specifically want, you're ready for the next step. The reprogramming process can be carried even further with visualization exercises and the help of motivational tapes.

Make a concerted effort to avoid all negatives; they're the obstacles you see when you take your eyes off the road you've decided to travel. At best, they slow you down. At worst, they can knock you completely off course.

With your thinking properly in gear, it is time to add action to the energy and emotion you've built.

The Flower Fund Fiasco

When Bruce Johnson told me I was promoted to vice-president of sales for Shamrock Broadcasting, my reaction was twofold: I was thrilled on one hand; scared to death on the other. You'll remember, I was still a relatively shy person at that time in my life. I hadn't yet advanced very far from the day I'd been asked to stand up in front of my fellow teachers and request that everyone donate five dollars to the flower fund. I literally froze. I could not get out of my seat to save my life.

When I was thirty-four years old a friend had asked me to accompany her to a lecture. There were only twelve people in the audience but when I was asked to introduce myself I simply could not do it. I couldn't even stand and simply give my name.

Then, no sooner did I find out that I was being elevated to vice-president of Shamrock than I received a letter from the National Association of Broadcasters, asking that I give a speech on how to increase sales, at the annual convention in Las Vegas.

This, bear in mind, was two short, frantic years after I had embarrassed myself at that lecture. I tried to find a way to turn down the NAB invitation gracefully, but there was no way. It finally dawned on me that I was going to have to do it. Somehow, I was going to walk out on a stage, look out at more than a thousand people, and give a forty-five-minute speech.

I had three months to prepare myself. It was time, I realized, to put the techniques I'd worked out into high gear. Over and over I visualized myself at the podium, giving that speech. I practiced; I polished; I saw myself as the professional equal of every other speaker on the program. I saw myself holding the attention of the audience.

I was visualizing myself in the present doing what I would be called on to do in the future.

Meeting Zig Ziglar

Having listened to his tapes for so long, I felt as if I knew Zig Ziglar personally. If anyone could help me become an overnight public speaker, it was Ziglar, one of the greatest motivational speakers of all time.

I began calling his office, then dropping by. Each time he was on the road or in a meeting. But I persisted until finally I was given an appointment.

That day I finally entered his office, it was almost on a dead run. He smiled and asked what he could do to help me.

"You're the one who got me into all this," I said. "Now you've got to help me." I ignored the puzzled look on his face and told him how helpful his tapes had been in bringing me out of my depression. I told him of my job with the health club, of my success as a salesperson at the radio station, of my new position as vice-president, and of the speech I was expected to give.

He listened as I went on and on about the things that had happened in my life since I had first heard his voice on tape. When I finally paused, he smiled and said, "Well, Miss Pam, you know I've always known that my tapes work. But I had no idea they worked that well!"

Aware that I'd never spoken to a group before, he offered me three basic tips:

1. Pick several people in the audience who are obviously responding to you and smiling at you as you're talking. Look at them; feed on their positive reaction. By doing so, you'll be getting positive reinforce-

ment that will help your own confidence and boost your self-image.

2. Don't look directly at anyone who has his arms crossed or who might be frowning. You can appear to be addressing them by looking just above their heads. On the other hand, never look up at the ceiling or behind you. Maintain eye contact with those in the audience who are giving you positive feedback and concentrate on them.

3. As you prepare for your speech, see yourself doing it perfectly, not forgetting a single line, never stumbling over a word. If you go over it enough in your mind, you will reach a point where visualizing it is much the same as actually giving the speech.

We talked for some time. Then, as I was preparing to leave, he reminded me once again about the importance of seeing myself doing well long before I actually had to give the speech.

"Just for kicks," he said, "add a standing ovation to your visualization. Have your audience on their feet, applauding, loving you."

I smiled and shrugged. "Why not?"

Ladies and Gentlemen . . .

As the time for the actual speech approached, I felt a growing sense of confidence. I'd gone over it so many times in my mind that subconsciously I was already looking upon myself as a seasoned speaker. I was certain I was not only going to get through the ordeal, but was going to make a definite contribution to the gathering.

It was a good thing I stepped to the lectern in a positive frame of mind. My notes had been carefully typewritten, but I had not realized that when you're addressing a large audience, trying to maintain eye contact, it is all but impossible to read from type so small. It is all but impossible to find your place again once you've lifted your eyes from the paper.

I was panic-stricken, but it was too late to back out. So I stepped away from the lectern and began to ad-lib. My long hours of practice enabled me to make the points I wanted to make without reference to my neatly typed speech. In truth, I knew it in my heart. I didn't need the crutch of a written text. I just told them in my own conversational style what I had done to raise sales and motivate the employees.

And it worked. I maintained eye contact, seeking out the friendly faces Zig Ziglar had told me I would find. They smiled. I smiled back. The more I smiled, the more others smiled. In time I was aware that virtually everyone in the audience was attentive and seemed to be enjoying what I had to say. It was a wonderfully rewarding feeling.

Then an even more remarkable thing occurred. As I finished my speech, people in the audience began to get to their feet as they applauded. I got the standing ovation Ziglar had told me to visualize.

In retrospect, there is just one thing I overlooked in my preparation for my debut as a public speaker. After it was over I returned to the hotel room, still a nervous wreck, and threw up.

The next time I made sure that not only did I visualize myself doing well and being well received, but I saw myself feeling good about what I'd done after it was over. However, for the next few days after the speech at the convention all the negative comments started pouring in. Broadcasters who had been in the industry for ten to twenty-five years came up to me and said, "You couldn't have become a vice-president of a major broadcasting chain in less than two years; that takes twenty years." I suddenly realized that had I thought it would take twenty years to become a vice-president, it *would* have taken me twenty years! Since I didn't know any better I did it in only two years.

The other favorite "negative" that surfaced was "You can't increase sales five hundred percent in one year after losing half of your station's audience." Again I thought to myself, "I'm glad I didn't know that before." Then they told me, "Your station can't be fifteenth in the ratings and third in local billing." I suddenly realized how glad I was that my sales staff and I didn't know that fact either. Everything they told me was "impossible." The only problem was that it was too late—I had already done it.

So that's where I get my slogan. And I give it to you to use the next time someone tells you that you can't accomplish or do the things that you dream about doing. You look them straight in the eye and say, "Don't tell me it's impossible until after I've already done it."

Failure Is the By-product of Worry

We devote a great deal of energy to, and undergo a lot of stress in, worrying about future failure. Forced into a position of having to make a speech, we too often spend more time convincing ourselves we're going to fail than we do visualizing success. It is proof of the False Evidence Appearing Real (FEAR) theory. If we worry enough about a future failure, we turn it into a self-fulfilling prophecy.

A person who dreads making a speech is sending an overload of negative signals to the subconscious. In turn, the subconscious is saying, "This lady wants to fail. She wants to forget her lines. She wants to appear nervous and unorganized." She worries ahead of time "Oh, no, I'll trip on stage." Later, when she actually is onstage, her subconscious will remember, "Lady wants to trip." Most likely she will. There is always a physical manifestation of the subconscious mind.

It is all too easy to program our minds with undue worry. Worry is, almost invariably, negative. It is a thought pattern that dwells on things we don't want to happen instead of what we do want. And by giving so much thought to the negative, we're practically assured of failure.

Worry, then, is an almost certain obstacle to goal setting.

There is a verse in the Bible (Mark 11:24) that says: "Therefore I say unto you, what things soever ye desire, when ye pray, believe that ye receive them, and ye shall have them." So what I'm suggesting isn't exactly new. Believing in the now will assure you of realizing your goals of the future. You visualize what you want to become and then move in that direction, gaining new momentum and confidence daily.

It is not nearly as mysterious as it may sound. If you constantly see yourself as having already reached a higher position in your profession, and adopt the actions and thoughts that go with that position, it will show. Your superiors will notice the change and begin to think maybe you're the person for that new vice-presidency. Next stop, a promotion. Why? Because you began to act like a person deserving that promotion.

Let's review: First, you have to have the picture in your mind. Then comes the action. That action will always fit the picture you've established. In time, others will see the change and you'll get additional positive response. Then you are even better able to believe you are the person you aspire to be.

Also, you see yourself doing in the present what you want of the future. That's when the dreams quit being just dreams and turn to reality.

15

When I was working as sales manager for radio station KMGC, I encouraged everyone on the staff to make a dream chart as part of the goal-setting process.

To make a dream chart, you find and clip out pictures of all the things you want to do and have: places you want to visit, clothes you'd like to wear, a home you wish you owned, even a person you'd like to meet. Of course it doesn't have to be the exact beach or suit or house; it doesn't even have to be the very person you are hoping to meet. But the pictures should be as close to the real thing in your mind as possible.

That's why I put my face on a picture of Farrah Fawcett when I was trying to lose weight. That's why I used a picture of the car I wanted so badly.

Your dream chart shouldn't stop at material things, however. If, for instance, your goal is to become more friendly, cut out pictures of people enjoying themselves at parties. You might even want to put your face on one who seems to be having a particularly good time. Then look at the picture every day, letting your mind accept the idea of a smiling, outgoing new you.

It isn't possible to make any real headway in changing your life until your mind accepts what you're trying to do. Show it pictures.

If We Had Known It Would Work This Well . . .

I once had everyone on my sales staff set goals for the upcoming year. Chuck wrote down the figure $30,000. Wayne decided he wanted to make $45,000. Throughout the year they saw those figures on their dream charts daily. The reminder of the goals they had set for themselves was there, over their desks, where they could see it every day as they came to the office.

Bear in mind, their income was based on commission. Some weeks will naturally be better than others during the course of a year. So it is pretty difficult, even by mid-year, to make a close estimate of what your total earnings will be.

Still, when they got their December checks, which showed the year-to-date earnings, they came running into my office. Both had made several hundred dollars more than the goals they had set for themselves.

And both agreed that if they had known it was going to work so well they would have set their goals higher.

One morning I walked into the sales room and found a picture of a deer on one salesman's dream chart. I sought Gary out and asked the obvious.

He smiled and informed me that deer season opened in a couple of weeks. "This year," he said, "I've decided I'm going to get the biggest deer I've ever bagged. I've written that on my chart. I'm going to make it happen."

Though I'm not really interested in hunting, I wished him luck and waited to see how things would turn out for him.

The Monday morning that he returned to work after his weekend hunting trip, there was a great deal of excitement in the office. Even before he got there, a clipping from the local paper had been tacked onto the bulletin board. There was Gary's picture in the sports section, accompanied by a story on his bagging of the largest deer in Texas on the opening day of the season.

Gary placed the article on his dream chart and wrote the word RESULTS across it in large, bold letters.

You wouldn't believe some of the things that went up on the dream charts of others after that.

In Gary's case, he made certain he was prepared to take full advantage of an opportunity when it presented itself. That deer was out there for every hunter who purchased a license, of course, but a hunter has only a split second when he sees that big deer he's dreamed of. How many didn't shoot quickly or accurately enough? How many simply froze because they had never seen a deer so large? They were not expecting such a situation to arise and therefore weren't ready when it did.

Gary, on the other hand, was prepared. He had stalked that deer in his mind again and again, making a perfect shot to bring the animal down. He had visualized a specific sequence of events, and when the mental images became reality, he simply carried out the actions he'd gone over in his mind. Which is to say, practice makes perfect, even if the practice is in your mind.

You Never Know Where a Wish Will Come True

Let me give you a few more examples:
One evening as I sat in my living room, it occurred to

me that a large plant would do wonders for a barren corner I had never been able to decide what to do with. What I wanted was a three-stalk cane yucca that would reach from floor to ceiling, about twelve feet. When I began checking prices, I found that plants of that size cost between $150 and $200. That, I knew, was out of my price range.

Checking my budget at the time, I determined that $40 was the maximum I could afford for any plant. Still, I was determined to have that three-stalk cane yucca. I even mentioned to a friend that I was going to keep looking until I found what I wanted at a price I could afford.

Less than a week later I was having my hair done, so late in the day that the shop had already closed, and only my hairdresser and the receptionist were left. As I sat there in my smock, my hair dripping wet, the receptionist came over to say that a man had just stuck his head in the front door and asked if anyone wanted to buy any plants.

"What kind of plants was he selling?"

"I don't know," the receptionist said. "He just said he has them in his van out in the parking lot."

My antenna went up immediately. Quickly excusing myself, I ran out into the parking lot, smock, dripping hair and all, and located the van. When the man opened the back doors I saw several of the most beautiful cane yucca plants I'd ever seen, each easily worth $200.

I asked the price of the particular one I wanted. "Lady," the salesman said, "I can let you have that one for forty dollars. But you've got to figure out how to get it home on your own."

I paid him on the spot and called a friend who owned a pickup.

Pure luck? Maybe. I prefer to think it was a combination of good fortune with specific and positive thinking.

Another time, shortly after my separation, I decided I needed a new bedroom set. After a little shopping I found exactly what I was looking for, but the price tag almost burned my hand. It was far more than I could afford. But it was the bed I wanted. I took the catalogue the salesman offered me, went home, and put the picture of that bed on the door of my refrigerator. For several days I visualized myself in that bed. In my mind I was already sleeping on it. Finally it became a reality—at half price. Somehow, I determined, I was going to get it.

The following week, I learned from one of my sales friends, the World Trade Center in Dallas was to host a furniture show. Now, to get into the Trade Center requires a special card given out to salespeople, designers, and special guests. I was none of the above but decided to drive out there anyway.

There would be, I knew, a great many security people, but dressed in my best business outfit, I felt I could bluff my way in. Looking confident and businesslike, I marched right past the security guards without being asked to show a card. The one guard I spoke with even gave me directions.

Taking the elevator, intuitively pushing the fifteenth floor button, I stepped off into one of the numerous furniture showrooms the massive building houses. And there, just a few feet away, was the bedroom set I was looking for in the showroom window. I was able to purchase it for less than half the retail price.

That would never have happened had I not made up my mind to find that bed at a reduced price, had I not been confident that I could get into the World Trade Center.

Of course, I wouldn't have you believe that such things happen all the time. But if you think they can, then work to make them happen, they do become possible. More often than you might think.

Watching for the Watch

Testimonials to the power of visualization are endless. And it always pleases me when people I've trained come to me with success stories of their own.

Here's the story of how the technique of visualization worked for a friend of mine:

When I first started trying to use the visualization methods, I was convinced they wouldn't work. It had always been my belief that a person had to work hard and save for long periods of time to get the material things he wants. But after I began going through the steps of visualization, I realized it was working for me, because I began to see the pictures in my mind. The more progress I made, the more firmly I believed in the approach.

During a visit to Palm Beach one summer, I visited an expensive jewelry store on Worth Street (something of an East Coast Rodeo Drive) and saw a beautiful gold watch. The price, needless to say, was several thousand dollars.

I wanted a watch like that. I made up my mind, standing there in the showroom, that I was going to have one, despite the fact I knew there was no way I could afford it. I decided this would be my ultimate test of the visualization process. I saw that watch in my mind almost constantly during the remainder of my stay.

Not only am I going to have a watch like that, I told myself, *but I'm going to have it in the very near future.* Such was the imprint on my mind.

As I flew back home on a Friday—without the watch, of course—I still had it on my mind. I thought about it during the trip, while I waited for my luggage, as I walked to the parking lot to get my car. That watch had become very important to me.

Before going home I stopped by the office to pick up my briefcase and some papers I needed to work on over the weekend before getting back to the office the following Monday. While I was there, gathering up the materials I needed, my supervisor came in, asked how my trip had been, then asked me to come into his office before I left. No sooner had he walked away, than I began to have stronger-than-ever feelings about the watch I'd seen in Palm Beach.

In his office we talked for several minutes. Then he said, "You've done an excellent job and I have something I want you to have as a token of my appreciation." He reached across his desk and handed me a blue velvet case.

I opened it—and there was my watch. I was speechless.

From that day forth, I have never doubted the powers of visualization.

Donahue Thanksgiving

After I had been in business for myself for some time, it occurred to me that additional media exposure would be of great benefit. Hoping to build a name for myself so that I might be invited to speak to a wider variety of audiences, I sought the help of a public relations man. But when he had been on the payroll for several months, I was still seeing no results. There was no evidence that he was sending out promotional kits, contacting magazines or newspapers, or, for that matter, even making any calls.

One morning as we discussed the problem, he mentioned a proposed Thanksgiving trip to California to visit his family. I suggested that while he was there, he check out the possibility of getting me on a television talk show.

"It would help," I told him, "if I could get on something like the Phil Donahue show."

A number of TV shows, as you know, have guests on a regular basis: the *Tonight Show, Merv Griffin, P.M. Magazine,* etc., but for some reason I kept using *Donahue* as my example.

The P.R. man carefully explained to me how difficult it was to get on one of the talk shows, pointing out that well-known celebrities are generally standing in line for such an opportunity.

Shortly thereafter I took a few days off, returning home on Thanksgiving Day. I called my answering service for any messages and was told that Zig Ziglar had phoned earlier in the day and said it was important that I get in touch with him.

The answering service had gotten the message wrong, I figured. Zig had probably called a day or so earlier. I was hesitant to interrupt him at home on Thanksgiving, and my first inclination was to wait until the holiday weekend was over. Finally, though, my curiosity got the better of me and I phoned him.

"Pam," he said, "I've agreed to be on the Phil Donahue show with Mary Kay Ash [of Mary Kay Cosmetics]. They're doing the show on motivation and asked if I would bring an additional guest. Would you be able to go?"

Would I be able to go!

The following Monday we were on a plane. On Tuesday we taped the show. After the taping, I called my public relations friend and told him the date he could see me on *Donahue.* For a moment, he was speechless.

"That's impossible," he said at last. "You've been giving speeches for less than six months. You're not really established yet. I know people who have been trying for years to get an invitation to be on that guy's show. And you really haven't even done anything yet."

But that was the very reason I had wanted to get on the show in the first place. Because I needed something: I needed the national exposure that would help me tell people who I am and what I do.

I'm not sure the public relations man ever understood my reasoning. By the same token, I could not understand his negative attitude.

16

In previous chapters we've talked about the necessity of changing the pictures in your mind before you actually take action toward achieving the goals you have set for the positive new you.

In this chapter, we'll focus on the visualization process, detailing an exercise that will help you expand those pictures in your mind.

A Fast Two-Hour Nap

One of the practical benefits of the visualization exercise that follows is that in only ten or fifteen minutes you can feel as rested as you might after a two-hour nap.

If, for instance, you're sitting in a reception area, nervously awaiting a job interview or sale, you can close your eyes and do a visualization exercise that will not only relax you but will program your mind for confidence during the interview. As you sit there waiting, picture yourself as already in the job you're seeking.

For another example, if you're at work and you get some disappointing news, you can simply place your head on your desk for a few minutes, relax, reprogram yourself into a more positive frame of mind, and go on about your work for the remainder of the day.

If you're tired and haven't had enough sleep, it can make you feel more rested in a few minutes' time. It is particularly effective if you can lie down.

If you're a mother who has had problems with the children during the day, you may fear your bad humor will spill over to the time when your husband gets home. Take a few minutes, put the trials of the day behind you, and visualize the warm reception you will give your spouse when he arrives.

In virtually any upsetting or discomforting confrontation, in fact, this exercise can help you relax, resolve the problem, and reprogram your mind in a more positive direction.

Many athletes are using visualization these days. A friend of mine who is an outstanding basketball player says he spends as much time visualizing the shots he's going to take in a game as he does in actual practice. Rafael Septien, the gifted kicker for the Dallas Cowboys, insists that when he goes onto the field to attempt a field goal, no matter from what distance, he has visualized thousands of times every movement that will be required of him. Golfers spend a great deal of time visualizing themselves' making a long birdie putt. Bowlers see the perfect game in their mind many times before they ever actually roll that 300.

By visualizing the kick or putt or winning shot at the buzzer, each athlete becomes more confident. They have already programmed their minds for the success that is to come.

I've heard stories of Vietnam prisoners of war who spent

five years playing mental golf. They would visualize themselves on a favorite course, playing it hole by hole, as a method of retaining their sanity and passing the endless hours. Then, once they got home, they found themselves playing better golf than they had before they left.

Since you never know when the opportunity will arise to use the visualization process, I suggest you read this chapter several times. Memorize it if necessary.

The Visualization Exercise

Get comfortable.

Turn down the lights.

If you want to lie on the bed or sofa or floor, that's fine.

Either put your head down or lean back—whichever is more comfortable for you.

Concentrate on becoming totally relaxed.

By doing these things at least once a day you are slowing down the brain waves. In order to get into your subconscious, it is necessary to accomplish that slowing-down process. Only then can you begin to reprogram your thought patterns into a more positive direction.

Once you feel relaxed, close your eyes, moisten your finger, and place a damp spot in the center of your forehead.

Concentrate on that spot until you have blocked everything else out of your mind.

Now, still relaxed, visualize yourself getting on an elevator on the tenth floor. You will then go to the ninth floor, relaxing even more as you make the descent. All the while you're going deeper into your mind, deeper into your subconscious, feeling yourself relax all over.

As you continue your downward journey, to the

eighth floor, you will feel a wave of relaxation beginning at your feet. Your feet will begin to feel so relaxed that you wouldn't be able to stand. Then your legs begin to relax in the same manner. The sensation then moves up over your chest, your neck and shoulders. You can feel all the muscles in your body relaxing.

The muscles in the back of your neck are relaxed; so are those in your head. You can feel your face relaxing, even your eyes. You'll feel something of a tingly sensation around your face and scalp.

As you go to the seventh floor, think about those things that are bothering you. Concentrate on the anxieties of the moment. Define them as completely as possible. What is the problem? What caused it? Why has it upset you so? It is impossible to get rid of something if you don't have it clearly defined.

So many times you may have worries and anxieties but really don't know what specifically is bothering you. Go on down to the sixth floor and think back to the time when, as a child, you felt the most insecure. Who were the people who caused that feeling? Let a picture of them come into your mind. Maybe they were people who loved you very much but put limitations on you, telling you "You can't do that" or "That's a foolish idea" or "You'll never succeed at that." See their faces and realize that *they* put those limitations on you. Then you will realize that the limitations are not yours but theirs. If you haven't already, get rid of those limitations. Toss out all the negatives and replace them with positive thoughts.

As you arrive at the fifth floor you'll find it totally surrounded by mirrors. Stop and look at yourself. Then decide which of the things you see that you want to change. Look at your weight, the manner in which you stand, the look on your face. What you're seeing is what others are going to see when they meet you for the first time. In a matter of minutes after that first meeting, they are going to form an opinion of you. And as we all know, first opinions are difficult to change. Look into those mirrors and determine what kind of first impression you are going to give others. You be the judge: Do you look as good as you really could?

Moving to the fourth floor, think of the person in your life who is most difficult to deal with. See yourself with that person and just relax. Sometimes we don't even realize who *is* difficult to deal with until we relax and take a good look. You may see more than one face, in fact. But, once those faces come to mind, ask yourself why you feel you're losing every time you're around them.

Then travel to the third floor. You're relaxing even more, seeing mental pictures of the things you've looked at on each floor you've visited. Let those pictures form in your mind as you continue down to the second floor, the first, and finally the basement.

Once you're there, the door opens and you walk out across a beautiful green meadow. The walk is peaceful and leads to steps leading down to a warm, inviting beach.

You walk down those steps, relaxing even more as you go—ten steps . . . nine steps . . . eight . . . seven . . . six . . . five . . . four . . . three . . . two . . . one, and you're on the beach. Feel the welcome warmth of the sun.

On the beach, you can hear the gentle sounds of the ocean and the seagulls. You're relaxing even more, letting all the negative energy leave your body. All anxieties, negative feelings about yourself, negative thoughts about others, worries, limitations; they're all gone.

They're going to rise up out of your body as another person and walk away toward the ocean. They're taking with them all the negative bindings that have held you down and caused you problems. You watch as they go farther and farther out to sea—until finally they have disappeared.

Now, through the top of your head feel the bright light of the sun coming in. That warm light represents positive energy.

As it comes in through the top of your head, feel it filling your head with positive thoughts. It's in your head now and you can feel it traveling down, going through your spine, touching all the nerves of your body, spreading positive energy throughout.

Feel the warmth and energy as it moves through your body, all the way to your toes. For the next few minutes you are going to be completely relaxed, filled with nothing but the positive bright light of the sun.

Now dream the biggest dream you've ever dared dream. Take all limitations off. Let your mind go as far as it can.

If you want a new car, see yourself in that car. If you want to take a vacation, see yourself in the greatest vacation spot you can imagine. If you want to trim down, see yourself at the weight you want to be. Don't just see yourself—see it happen through your own eyes. Feel yourself in the car or on the vacation.

Pick what you want in the future but imagine yourself as having already attained it—now, this very minute.

Relax again but allow your mind to continue exploring new horizons. Assume there are no boundaries to your fantasies, your imagination. Let your mind go and just have fun for a few minutes.

Now imagine that the elevator you came down in earlier is right there on the beach. Get on, and as you climb from the basement to the first floor you are still relaxed but you feel your energy returning. The negativity is gone and you feel more energized than you've ever felt.

When you get to the second floor, consider how positive you've begun to feel.

At the third, feel the energy in your mind and the power you suddenly have to accomplish those things in life you want.

At the fourth floor, see that person that was most difficult for you to deal with, but now see yourself in control of yourself and handling any situation that might arise.

When you get to the fifth floor, look in those mirrors again and see yourself as the person you want to be; smiling, cheerful, the proper weight, dressed sharply. Perfect.

On the sixth floor, see yourself getting a paycheck that is five times larger than any you've ever received. See yourself going to the bank, opening a savings account, then purchasing some of the things you've wanted but didn't feel you could afford.

On the seventh floor, feel yourself in that new car you've been wanting. See the color, hear the stereo playing, feel the power of the motor. Drive past a building with a big plate-glass window. Stop and look at the reflection of you in your new car.

At the eighth floor, visualize yourself doing things for others, sharing, loving, giving.

On floor nine think of the short-term goals you had decided on that day and see them as already accomplished.

And at the tenth floor, think of the long-term goals you've decided on. Think of them accomplished as well, successfully, perfectly.

Now, slowly count from one to ten, and as you get

closer to ten, feel yourself refreshed, as if you've had a two-hour nap.

When you hear yourself say "ten" in your mind, open your eyes and look at a new world.

And go after those goals.

Summary

Now it's up to you. No book, speech, or taped message is going to make you magically into the person you want to be—unless you have the desire to take the first important steps necessary to setting change into motion.

This book is nothing more than a guideline, a suggested starting place. If it gets you on the road to a richer, more satisfying and rewarding life, it has achieved its purpose. And I shall not be so modest as to suggest I'm not pleased. At the same time, if you do reach the levels of success you now aspire to, the victory is yours.

Again, bear in mind that those changes and successes you desire aren't going to come overnight. Nor are they achieved without a large measure of hard work, determination—and a stumble or two along the way.

By the same token, you'll not begin getting close to them until the moment you decide to take that first step.

The best start I know is to get acquainted with yourself. Determine, through some honest self-evaluating questions, just who you are and who you wish to become.

On the following pages are some exercises that will get you under way. Read them carefully; then think seriously about them before you answer the questions or fill in the lists.

Most important, look them over after you've finished. Not once, but several times. You'll be amazed at what you've told yourself. What you'll find by careful evaluation of your responses is a road map to your own success and happiness.

Good luck.

May all your dreams come true. God bless you.

List ten unusual experiences from your childhood that make you unique:

1.

2.

3.

4.

5.

6.

7.

8.

9.

10.

List the five things in your life you're proudest of:

1.

2.

3.

4.

5.

List six life-changing events that you have experienced:

1.

2.

3.

4.

5.

6.

What strange things have happened to you that are difficult to explain?

1.

2.

3.

4.

5.

6.

7.

8.

9.

10.

List five unusual things you were hesitant at first to try but managed to succeed at:

1.

2.

3.

4.

5.

What is special, unique, and different about you that can help you to become more successful?

  1.

  2.

  3.

  4.

  5.

  6.

  7.

  8.

  9.

 10.

What are the things about yourself that you most want to change?

  1.

  2.

  3.

  4.

  5.

  6.

List ten things you are going to put on your dream chart (and think big!):

1.

2.

3.

4.

5.

6.

7.

8.

9.

10.

Write three stories of approximately two pages each, detailing fantasies you would like to have come true (and don't be afraid to get a little far-out):

Write a paragraph about your most embarrassing moment or biggest failure:

Now write a paragraph about your biggest success or the happiest moment in your life:

Fill out the following lists to determine the mental prison you've locked yourself in:

Negative Beliefs You Have About Yourself	Source of Beliefs (other people, events, yourself, etc.)
1.	1.
2.	2.
3.	3.
4.	4.
5.	5.

List the things that will help you in your escape to freedom:

Positive Beliefs You Have About Yourself	Source of Beliefs (other people, events, yourself, etc.)
1.	1.
2.	2.
3.	3.
4.	4.
5.	5.

What five negative behavior patterns do you have now that you would most like to change?

Negative Behavior Patterns	What I Want To Be
1.	1.
2.	2.
3.	3.
4.	4.
5.	5.

Goal Planning Guide

Start at the bottom of the triangle, filling in each box as you work your way to the top, concluding with the benefits to you. And remember, obstacles are what you see when you take your eyes off your goals.

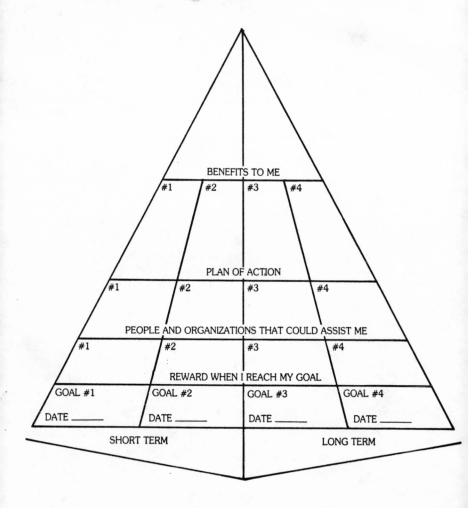

Final Words of Advice

1. Face the truth about yourself.
2. Decide what you want from life, then see short-term and long-term goals.
3. Be specific.
4. Avoid the negative.
5. Reprogram your mind daily with motivational cassette tapes as well as inspirational and educational books.
6. Do the visualization exercise in your mind for ten minutes daily.
7. See yourself as achieving something—now.
8. Make a dream chart.
9. Make up your mind to believe you can accomplish your goals.
10. Apply the appropriate action to whatever situation you're in.
11. Believe in your own higher power or God, whoever that is to you.
12. Don't let anyone tell you it's impossible until after you've already done it!

Self-help Audio Cassettes by Pam Lontos

"How to Program Yourself for Success in 30 Days"
"Think Yourself Thin Forever"
"Cash In on Your Dreams" (8-hour sales)
"Tune Into Success in Broadcast Sales"

Video Training
Twelve-Session Video Motivation and Sales Course

For additional information, write:
Lontos Sales & Motivation, Inc.
P.O. Box 1047
Carpinteria, California 93013
Or call: (805) 684-6953